The Story of Guadalupe

Nahuatl Studies Series
Number 5

Series Editor
James Lockhart
Associate Series Editor
Rebecca Horn

UCLA Latin American Studies
Volume 84

The Story of Guadalupe

Luis Laso de la Vega's
Huei tlamahuiçoltica
of 1649

edited and translated by

Lisa Sousa
Stafford Poole, C.M.
James Lockhart

Stanford University Press

UCLA Latin American Center Publications
University of California, Los Angeles

Stanford University Press
Stanford, California

CIP data appear at the end of the book

Contents

Introduction

THE DEVOTION to Our Lady of Guadalupe is one of the most important elements in the development of a specifically Mexican tradition of religion and nationality over the centuries. The picture of the *Virgen morena* (Dark Virgin) is to be found everywhere throughout the republic of Mexico, and her iconography is varied almost beyond telling. Though innumerable books, both historical and devotional, have been printed on the topic in this century alone, it is only recently that the textual sources of the devotion have been closely studied or even made available to the general reader.[1]

In the version of the legend most widely spread today, the Virgin appeared in 1531 at Tepeyacac (modern Tepeyac) just north of Mexico City, leading in short order to the establishment of a shrine there. Yet as a thorough study by one of our number[2] has shown, no texts can be found for the apparition story as it is now divulged that go back earlier than the middle of the seventeenth century. We do know that a chapel dedicated to the Virgin of Guadalupe existed at the Tepeyacac site by the 1550's. It is to that decade that the first known mentions of the matter attribute an apparition of the Virgin; the relevant passages, however, are few, brief, ambiguous, and themselves posterior by many years. Not until much later did the now current story of the 1531 events establish itself and gain countrywide recognition. Another of us, in a study involving an extensive survey of Nahuatl texts of all kinds, found few references to Guadalupe until the second half of the seventeenth century.[3]

The nature and the popularity of the Guadalupe legend thus seem to have been strongly affected by two texts that Mexican-born Spanish ecclesiastics published in the late 1640's. The earlier of the two was in Spanish. In 1648 Miguel Sánchez, a diocesan priest of Mexico City, came out with a book entitled *Imagen de la Virgen Maria, Madre de Dios de Guadalupe*,[4] containing the first presently known account of the Mexican appearances of

---

[1]De la Maza 1981; de la Torre Villar and Navarro de Anda 1982; O'Gorman 1986; Nebel 1992; Noguez 1993; Poole 1995.

[2]Poole 1995.

[3]Lockhart 1992. The contents of the present publication supersede the brief and provisional analysis of Laso de la Vega's work set forth there.

[4]Miguel Sánchez 1648. It is reproduced in de la Torre Villar and Navarro de Anda 1982, pp. 152–281, and with some omissions in López Beltrán 1981 (IVM). Relevant extracts are translated below in Appendix 2.

the Virgin of Guadalupe. Here we see the full story as it is repeated to this day. In Sánchez's tale, the Virgin appeared on the hill of Tepeyacac, outside Mexico City, to a Nahua commoner named Juan Diego and sent him to the bishop-elect of Mexico, fray Juan de Zumárraga, with instructions to have a church built on that site in her honor. The bishop (for so he is considered in the story) was skeptical of Juan Diego's message but was eventually persuaded to ask for a sign confirming it. In response, the Virgin had Juan Diego go to the top of the hill, where he found roses blooming out of season in a place where they would ordinarily not grow. He picked the flowers, wrapped them in his mantle, and took them to the bishop. When he unfolded the garment in the bishop's presence, the roses cascaded to the floor, and on the cloak a picture of the Virgin was left imprinted. Asking forgiveness for his skepticism, the bishop immediately undertook the construction of a small chapel at Tepeyacac.

Sánchez was the first person to make known the story of the apparitions, and for long afterward, as the shrine and the image began to become the focal point of Mexican religious and national life, his version had primacy. Beginning in the eighteenth century, however, his account was gradually eclipsed by that of Luis Laso de la Vega, the vicar of Guadalupe, so that in more recent times the latter version has come to be regarded by many as the seminal record, reaching back to the very time of the miracles. Laso de la Vega's account was published in 1649 in Nahuatl under the title *Huei tlamahuiçoltica omonexiti in ilhuicac tlatocacihuapilli Santa Maria totlaço-nantzin Guadalupe in nican Huei altepenahuac Mexico itocayocan Tepeyacac* (By a Great Miracle the Heavenly Queen, Saint Mary, Our Precious Mother of Guadalupe, Appeared here near the Great Altepetl of Mexico, in a Place called Tepeyacac).[1] It had the Nahuas (and perhaps ecclesiastics conversant with Nahuatl) as its intended readership, unlike Sánchez's work, which was directed primarily to the locally born Spaniards of Mexico City, whom we may call *criollos* if we remain cognizant of the limitations of the term, and how relatively infrequently it was then used in the meaning we now tend to give it.[2] The basic story as told in the *Huei tlamahuiçoltica* agrees closely

---

[1]Lasso de la Vega 1649.

[2]The term "criollo," which originated among the Portuguese, was first applied only to Africans born outside Africa. Gradually it was extended to other people, including Indians, who were born outside their traditional homeland. Most of those whom it described were on the humble end of the scale. Before the end of the sixteenth century Spanish-born Spaniards began to call native-born Spaniards criollos, usually by way of insult. Bit by bit those insulted began to turn the term around and use it as a slogan. They did

with Sánchez's version, in its facts, sequence, episodes, and main characters: the benevolent Virgin, the initially reluctant bishop, and above all the naive, transparent, but quite eloquent Juan Diego. The only noticeable substantive difference is the omission of the third of the four apparitions in Sánchez's story, and that episode is relatively secondary even there. But despite the basic similarity, the impression given by the two accounts is starkly different. In Sánchez, the story proper occupies short paragraphs between long sections of biblical analogy to which few modern readers respond sympathetically. In Laso de la Vega's story, the biblical material is entirely missing, creating a charming simplicity of line, and in compensation the dialogue is much more fully developed, in the normal fashion of Nahuatl compositions of various kinds. It is to its literary or dramatic qualities, as well as to the growing feeling over time that the indigenous aspect was central and original, that Laso de la Vega's version owes its ascendancy.

Its importance notwithstanding, the *Huei tlamahuiçoltica* of 1649 was not reprinted until 1926. In that year Primo Feliciano Velázquez published a facsimile of the original work and an excellent Spanish translation.[3] Since then there have been several translations into Spanish of the central apparition story, but none of the entire book. Translations into English have been on a popular level.[4] There is no scholarly English translation of

---

so sparingly and slowly, however, and normally they were simply *españoles*, "Spaniards." Blacks and Indians continued to be called criollo, and the term "criollo de" meant local in a given place, being used not only of people but of plants and animals. By the later eighteenth century, "Spaniard" undefined tended to mean native-born Spaniard, what we call a criollo, while the Spanish-born Spaniards were qualified as "European" or "peninsular," or called *gachupines* (a term of insult apparently coming from Nahuatl).

[3]Lasso de la Vega 1926 (HT).

[4]Lamadrid 1991 reproduces the *Nican mopohua* as found in Laso de la Vega 1649, but does not include a new translation. The transcription uses modern orthography, and there is no attempt to reproduce the diacritics. Rojas Sánchez 1978 also reproduces the *Nican mopohua* text with modernized orthography and gives a new translation. This version has gained great popularity in Mexico. The transcription is included in Nebel 1995. Lamadrid 1991 reproduces the paraphrase of Luis Becerra Tanco, and the translations of Velázquez, Angel María Garibay (unpublished), and Rojas Sánchez in parallel columns. The *Nican mopohua* has been translated into English in Cawley 1983; this is a poetic version, though the original Nahuatl is in prose, and it varies from literal to paraphrase. Demarest and Taylor 1956 (reprinted 1959), pp. 39–53, includes an English translation of Lorenzo Botturini Benaduci's Spanish version of the *Nican mopohua*.

the apparition story and none at all of the entire *Huei tlamahuiçoltica*.

The present edition seeks to remedy the situation by offering a faithful transcription of the complete text of the 1649 book, together with a translation and critical apparatus.[1] We hope to serve three main purposes. The first is to give the English speaking public access to a version of the texts which will be easily readable and reveal their true qualities. The second is to provide advanced students of Nahuatl with an annotated, readily usable transcription and translation of what is, although not so intended, surely one of the best works ever produced for learning the refinements of the older form of the Nahuatl language. The third (partly overlapping with the second) is to advance the philological analysis of the texts, trying to penetrate deeper into the nature of the words and expressions, not only in order to comprehend the meaning better, but to try to find out more about the work's affinities and authorship. This process has led to provisional results some of which we ourselves would hardly have predicted, pointing on the one hand to an extremely close relationship between the texts of the *Imagen de la Virgen Maria* and the *Huei tlamahuiçoltica*, as different as the two seem at first glance, and on the other hand to a very strong role of Laso de la Vega himself in the composition of the Nahuatl work, going against our expectation that the person primarily responsible for the final version of an ecclesiastical text in older Nahuatl would have been an indigenous aide (or aides).

Delving into these matters soon involves one in highly technical considerations of philology and grammar, and we are fully aware that some of our readers, especially those corresponding to our first purpose, will not wish to accompany us all the way through this preliminary study. Let us therefore first say what will be found in the following pages, so that readers will have some sense of what they are choosing or avoiding, as the case may be. In the immediately following section, we speak at length of the structure and general characteristics of the *Huei tlamahuiçoltica*, especially

---

[1]For purposes of transcription we initially used the facsimile published in the Velázquez edition. To remedy some gaps and unclarities in the facsimile, we had recourse to a copy of the original in the John Carter Brown Library, leading to the discovery that though the facsimile is overwhelmingly correct, it is not reliable. Some of the gaps in it were caused by the photographic process and are not to be observed in the original; many unclear letters and diacritics are distinct in the original. Above all, someone attempted to fill in gaps in the facsimile by hand, sometimes committing serious errors. We have relied primarily on inspection of a microfilm of the original kindly provided by the Library, supplemented by a personal inspection of some crucial passages in the actual original by Kevin Terraciano, to whom we are thankful.

in comparison with the work of Miguel Sánchez. The next section expands upon the notion that despite the apparent diversity or even disparity of the different parts of the book, they do have many aspects of unity, indicating the involvement of the same person or team throughout. Following sections deal with evidence of Spanish language influence and with some complex orthographic matters, both of which, in addition to their interest in themselves, bear importantly on the theme of unity. The next section discusses the way certain terms and expressions are used in the work, from large topics requiring several paragraphs to words discussed very succinctly. For students of the language, this part can serve to some extent as a work-specific glossary; it also offers us an opportunity to discuss our methods and conventions of translation. A final section reviews the evidence on the question of the authorship of the texts.

The structure of the *Huei tlamahuiçoltica* and its affinities with the work of Miguel Sánchez

THE WORK considered as a whole—and not merely the apparition story, to which popular interest often reduces it—is a complex agglomeration of sharply distinct parts. They can be considered from three different perspectives, each with its own significance. A part is defined in one way, possibly the most meaningful, by internal evidence: a style and subject matter of its own, some structure or order complete in itself. In the original printed book, parts are also defined or ignored typographically, by putting the headings in type of a certain size and beginning the section with a new page or not. A third way of determining parts is to check whether or not the section has a close parallel in the publication of Miguel Sánchez. Sections that do may have originated with Sánchez or some text common to Sánchez and Laso de la Vega, and at the very least are likely to be reworkings of something already existing, whereas sections without such a parallel would seem more likely to have been written entirely new for Laso de la Vega's publication. The parts we can distinguish are as follows:

1. The preface, phrased as a prayer to the Virgin. The section necessarily begins with a new page, and also ends on a page all to itself. In it Laso de la Vega speaks in the first person, and his name even appears at the end. The vocabulary and syntax are more elaborate than that found in the immediately following story proper, and there are biblical allusions, lacking in the story and the miracles. The section seems like an equivalent of the Latinate, allusive prefaces that ecclesiastics composed for all their works. This part lacks a close parallel in Sánchez.

2. The account of the apparitions, called the *Nican mopohua* ("Here is re-

counted") from its opening words. The section again begins with a new page; the lettering is even larger than that at the heading of the preface, clearly indicating that the body of the work begins here. This part is in an elevated Nahuatl and thus quite complex at times, but much less so than the preface. Its technique gives great prominence to dialogue, and its language is mainly that of polite Nahuatl conversation. Virtually all of the substance parallels Sánchez closely. The section ends thematically with the public acclaim of the miraculous image, but it is not set off typographically from what follows.

3. A description of the image as it was displayed in the shrine at Tepeyacac in Laso de la Vega's time, continuing without a page break or new heading. Going into great concrete detail and containing no dialogue, it is very different in style from the preceding story. Certain peculiarities of its language, of which the repeated use of the modal auxiliary -*ticac* (to stand doing something) leaps out, in all probability simply reflect its subject matter.[1] Again, the content and organization of nearly the entire section is closely paralleled in Sánchez (Appx. 2, pp. 139–40). An important typographical break comes at the end of this part, so that in the book it is in effect presented as part of the apparitions story, or at most as a coda to it.

4. A collection of fourteen miracle stories connected with the image, known from its opening words as the *Nican motecpana* ("Here is an ordered account"). The letters in the heading announce a major division by their size and boldness, but are considerably smaller and less elaborate than those in the heading of the *Nican mopohua*. Not starting a new page, the section is somewhat subordinated to the apparitions story proper. The style is generally more matter-of-fact, less dialogued, than in the *Nican mopohua*, but there are internal distinctions. Some of the first miracles are quite elaborately worked up, and one even has a speech not unlike those found in the story proper, but several of the other episodes are brief and quite perfunctory. More Spanish loanwords are found here than in any other part of the book. A large portion of this section is paralleled in Sánchez, not only in the content but also in the order of the episodes. Episodes continue, however, which are not in Sánchez, though most are mentioned in an engraving circulating in Mexico City in the early seventeenth century, and one has close parallels in the writing of the Franciscan chronicler Mendieta.[2] This part is not distinguished typographically from the following one.

---

[1]It appears that the -*ticac* modal was standardly used in describing images. See AC, f. 54v, where of an image of San Nicolás de Tolentino it is said that "cītlallòtìcac," "it stands [is] full of stars."

5. The further life of Juan Diego. Nothing about the printing distinguishes this section from the miracle stories, to which in the externals it belongs, perhaps again as a coda. It constitutes a relatively brief hagiography in the manner of the Spanish saints. There is no dialogue; the style seems to be simply what is dictated by the content. This portion is not closely paralleled in Sánchez, though two widely separated paragraphs there could be viewed as containing its germ.[3]

6. An exhortation to devotion to Guadalupe and an account of the history of the Virgin in New Spain generally, known from its opening words as the *Nican tlantica* ("Here ends"). It does not begin a new page; large letters accentuate the beginning of a new section, but they are fewer in number than at the beginning of the *Nican motecpana*, and most of them are in lower case. At the end of this part comes "Laus Deo," indicating the end of the body of the work. Typographically, then, this section could be taken to be integrated into the *Nican motecpana*. Insofar as it consists of post-apparition historical matter, it fits that position thematically, but as an exhortation it is more like the preface. It resumes something of the tone of the preface, reverting to complex syntax, going into theological matters, quoting a Latin Christian text, talking as the preface does about the workings of time. Laso de la Vega does not appear overtly in the first person here as he does there, but still the reader gets the impression that he is again speaking to us directly. The *Nican tlantica* has no close parallel in Sánchez's work.

7. A concluding prayer, written as a loose paraphrase of the Hail, Holy Queen (*Salve, Regina*). Set on a new page, on which the entire prayer fits, it has a heading reminiscent of those of the Spanish evaluation and license which precede the Nahuatl work. It is thus set off from the rest as something ancillary, a text for believers to memorize and recite more than a new communication to them. Sánchez has no parallel to the prayer.

Of the seven sections here laid out, three, constituting the core of the work, coincide to a large extent with material in Sánchez's book. Seeing that Sánchez's volume appeared first, that his work was known and admired by Laso de la Vega, who expressed his praise inside the covers of Sánchez's

---

[2]Poole 1995, pp. 85–87; Mendieta 1971, 3: 347–52. Poole shows that a parallel account attributed by some to the historian don Fernando de Alva Ixtlilxochitl actually derives from the *Huei tlamahuiçoltica* itself.

[3]Appx. 2, p. 141. Juan Diego's testamentary provisions actually differ in substance in Sánchez and Laso de la Vega. In Sánchez the fragments of Juan Diego's life come before the miracles; in Laso de la Vega, as we see above, the life comes after the miracles.

book itself, and that no earlier version of the story proper or the image description is known (nor does Sánchez refer to any), it is natural to imagine that Laso de la Vega was basing himself to a large extent directly on Sánchez. Direct dependence cannot be strictly proved, but one can at least examine the two texts to see if such a relationship was possible, and how it could have worked.

As seen above, Sánchez's version interpolates a vast amount of biblical analogy, overwhelming the narrative in the narrower sense. Even his narrative proper contains some elaborate vocabulary in what we could loosely call the Spanish baroque style. Let us imagine all this deleted. What is left would contain all the essential elements of the story as it appears in Laso de la Vega, but in a strangely truncated form, for Sánchez does not tell most of the encounters between Juan Diego and the bishop directly, presenting only what Juan Diego said to the Virgin, which does include a full account of what passed in the encounters. Such a procedure can be understood in a Spanish composition, for older Spanish tended to economize in matters of narrative and conversational detail.

Suppose that Laso de la Vega was attempting to do Sánchez's tale in the Nahuatl manner. Older Nahuatl accounts insisted on complete (or complete appearing) reproduction of all speeches. Original speeches were given in full, and when a speaker transmitted what was said to a third party, virtually the entire speech, in first person, was repeated. Laso de la Vega would thus be expected to reconstruct the original encounters between Juan Diego and Zumárraga, repeating them almost word for word in Juan Diego's reports to the Virgin. That is in fact what we find. The reconstruction would pose no problem, for Juan Diego's accounts to the Virgin in Sánchez are comprehensive.

Imagining the process in this fashion, we can account for the bulk of the content of the *Nican mopohua*. But not all of it. The strings of honorific vocatives at the beginning and ending of speeches, the frequent examples of polite small talk, the metaphorical double phrases are not to be found in Sánchez. They do not, however, add anything of substance to the tale, and sources for them were readily available, whether in refined Nahuatl conversation or in well known Nahuatl texts of ecclesiastical provenience. Such collections as the Bancroft Dialogues, the *Huehuetlatolli* of fray Juan Bautista, Book Six of the Florentine Codex, or various sets of biblical/moralistic plays,[1] all of which were in some form circulating in Mexico at

---

[1]See ANS; Bautista 1988; Sahagún 1950–82, part 7 (Book 6); Horcasitas 1974.

this time, contain models for virtually every example of Nahuatl rhetoric used in the Guadalupe texts. This was conventional material and common property. Many of the formulations were still part of living speech in the first half of the seventeenth century, at least in the upper levels of Nahua society and on formal occasions,[2] but examples become rarer as time goes on. One may doubt that the elaborate strings of metaphorical vocatives were still current, making it all the more likely that the copious ecclesiastical texts, often used for instructional purposes by such pedagogues as Carochi, were the source.

A single model was employed for the speech of all the characters. The Virgin, Juan Diego, and the bishop (who, however, has much less to say) all use the same elevated Nahuatl, the same rhetorical devices. It is indeed Juan Diego's combination of a disarming simplicity and conventional polite, cultivated speech that gives him such appeal. The effect is much more pronounced in Laso de la Vega's version than in Miguel Sánchez's, but it is not entirely lacking there either, as when Juan Diego on parting from the Virgin says "quédate en buenas horas," approximately "and I wish you good day."

The end result of the compositional process bears a good deal of resemblance to Nahuatl ecclesiastical plays or to the conversational/rhetorical collections,[3] but they consist entirely of speeches, whereas in the Guadalupe story, no matter how central the dialogue, third person narrative is equally essential. Though consisting of elements familiar in the Spanish and the Nahuatl traditions, the Laso de la Vega publication remains unique in the history of ecclesiastical Nahuatl philology.

To make clearer the relationship between the Sánchez and Laso de la Vega versions of the Guadalupe story, let us hold up against each other their accounts of a single episode, Juan Diego's interview with the Virgin after first seeing the bishop.[4] Material that corresponds closely is italicized for easier visibility. For the reader's convenience, we include here only English translations of the passages; the original Spanish and Nahuatl will be found in facing columns in Appendix 1.

Sánchez	Laso de la Vega
The same day he returned with the reply, and *climbing up to the*	*He came back* right away, *on the* very *same day. He came* straight *to*

---

[2]See Lockhart 1991, pp. 66–87.
[3]A resemblance already noted in García Icazbalceta n.d.
[4]IVM, pp. 80–81 (Appx. 2, pp. 132–33); below, pp. 68–71.

assigned place on that *mountain,* the trustworthy messenger, Juan Diego, finding the *Virgin* Mary mercifully *awaiting him, humbling himself in her presence* with all the forms of reverence *said to her,*

Lady and Mother, *I obeyed your command; not without travail I went in to visit the bishop,* at whose feet I knelt down. *He received me mercifully,* blessed me lovingly, *listened to me* attentively, and gave a lukewarm *answer, saying to me,* "Son, *you may come another day* when it is appropriate; *I will listen* to your claim *more deliberately* and *will get to the root of this mission of yours." I judged by* his appearance and *his words that he was persuaded* that the petition about *the temple that you ask him to build in your name in this place* was born *of my own imagination and not of your order,* for which reason I *implore you to charge another* person, *who will be credited* more, with such a matter.

the top of the hill and found the heavenly *Lady* in the same place where he first saw her, *waiting for him.* When he saw her, *he bowed low before her* and threw himself to the ground, *saying to her*:
My patron, O personage, *Lady,* my youngest child, my daughter, I went to where you sent me, *I went to carry out your instructions.* Although it was *difficult* for me to *enter* the quarters of *the priestly ruler,* I did see him, and I put before him your message as you ordered me to. *He received me kindly and heard it out,* but when *he answered me,* he did not seem to be satisfied or convinced. *He told me, "You are to come again, and I will hear you at leisure. First I will thoroughly look into what you have come about,* your wish and desire." *I could* easily *see from how he answered me that he thought that perhaps I was just making it up that you want them to build a temple there for you and that perhaps it is not by your order.* I greatly *implore you,* patron, noble Lady, my daughter, *entrust* one of the high nobles, who are recognized, respected, and honored, to carry and take your message, *so that he will be believed.* For I am a poor ordinary man, I carry burdens with the tumpline and carrying frame, I am one of the common people, one who is governed. Where you are sending me is not my usual place, my daughter, my youngest child, O personage, O Lady. Pardon me if

There will be no lack of many, *answered* the most holy Virgin, *but it is necessary that you negotiate it* and that *my desire* should succeed *at your hands*. I ask, charge, and *implore you to return tomorrow* with the same concern *to the bishop* and *on my behalf to require him and notify him of my will so that the house I ask of him will be built, repeating to him decidedly that it is I, the Virgin MARY, mother of God, who send you.*

I cause you concern, if I incur or bring upon myself your frown or your wrath, O personage, O my Lady.

The revered consummate Virgin *answered him,*
Do listen, my youngest child. Be assured that my servants and messengers to whom I entrust it to carry my message and realize my wishes are not high ranking people. Rather *it is* highly *necessary that you yourself be involved* and take care of it. It is very much *by your hand that my will and wish are to be carried out* and accomplished. I strongly *implore you,* my youngest child, and I give you strict orders that *tomorrow you* be sure to *go see the bishop once again. Instruct him on my behalf, make him fully understand my will and wish, so that he will carry out the building of my temple that I am asking him for.* And be sure to *tell him again how it is really myself, the ever Virgin Saint Mary, the mother of God the deity, who is sending you there.*

Juan Diego *answered her, saying to her,*
My patron, O Lady, my daughter, let me not cause you concern, for *with all my heart I will go there and carry out your message.* I will not abandon it under any circumstances; although I find *the road* painful, I will go to do your will. The only thing is that *I may not be heard out, or when I have been heard I may not be believed.*

My lady, Juan said to her, with much pleasure, care, and punctuality *I will obey the order you have given me,* so that you should not think that I refuse the effort, *the road,* or the fatigue. *I do not know if they will want to hear me, and when they hear me, if they will decide to believe me.* I will see you *tomorrow when the sun is setting*; then *I will return with the second decision of* the bishop. *I am going; I wish you good day.*

However, *tomorrow*, late in the afternoon, *when the sun is going down, I will come returning whatever answer the priestly ruler should give me* to your message. Now, my youngest child, my daughter, O personage, O Lady, *I am taking leave of you;* meanwhile, *take your rest.*

Note that the portions present in Laso de la Vega and missing in Sánchez, causing the considerably greater length of the former, add nothing to the narrative substance. They are accounted for almost entirely by honorific vocatives, polite apologies, and conventional Nahuatl metaphorical phrases referring to social rank. The rest is closely parallel not only in overall content but in sequence. Not all cognate portions of the two books are so close, but our selection indicates the nature of the correspondence. Other particularly close parallels are found in the description of the image and in the wording of the episode where the bishop sends his people to follow Juan Diego.

Indeed, if we accept the notion of direct dependence, some passages in Sánchez can be used to explain and even help translate parallel passages in Laso de la Vega. In the attempt to spy on Juan Diego,[1] Sánchez's phraseology explains why the other text uses a "not only . . . but" construction and throws light on if not resolves the question of the meaning of "quitlahuellalilique." This form at first glance looks as though it would mean something like "they threw him in a bad light, made him look bad." Under close morphological analysis, however, such an interpretation cannot stand up. Yet when we see that at the corresponding spot Sánchez has "desacreditandolo," we must suspect that the first glance corresponds to Laso de la Vega's intention, and that the form is one of his various slips (see below). In Juan Diego's climactic interview with the bishop (p. 84), the word *yeppa* occurs in connection with his seeing the Virgin on top of the hill, and one hesitates whether to translate the word as "before, previously" or "always." It is suggestive that in the corresponding place Sánchez (IVM, p. 92) has *siempre*, "always." The same effect can be seen in the miracles section. In the third of the miracles, Laso de la Vega's text has the strange phrase "nican omentin tlaca," "here two people," where we may wonder if the inten-

---

[1]Below, pp. 72–75; IVM, p. 85 (Appx. 2, p. 134).

tion is not "omentin nican tlaca," "two here-people, two indigenous people." On the corresponding spot Sánchez (IVM, p. 172) has "dos Indios," strengthening if not absolutely confirming the initial suspicion. In Laso de la Vega (p. 102 below), the phrase "çã çemi" (often meaning "once for all" or the like) in relation to miracles worked by the Virgin is puzzling, open to various interpretations. We may suspect that we have come at the root intention when we read in Sánchez (IVM, p. 175; Appx. 2, p. 144) at the appropriate place "en vn milagro tantos milagros," "so many miracles in one."

Following the story proper, the first six miracles narrated by Laso de la Vega and Sánchez correspond in both content and order. Sánchez's seventh miracle describes the flooding of Mexico City and is not present in Laso de la Vega, conceivably because even in Sánchez's presentation the events do not seem very decisive or miraculous. On the other hand, Laso de la Vega's seventh miracle, not in Sánchez's miracle list, does parallel very closely a separate description in Sánchez of the healing power of the fountain at the shrine (Appx. 2, pp. 140–41). After this, Laso de la Vega's text adds another seven miracles not in Sánchez. The eighth through thirteenth miracles give skeletal representations of cures at the shrine. Most of these episodes, though not in Sánchez, are in an early seventeenth-century engraving by Samuel Stradanus (as are some of the ones shared by Laso de la Vega and Sánchez, for that matter).[1] The correspondence between Laso de la Vega, Sánchez, and Stradanus is complex, perhaps most easily grasped through tabulation. Table 1 gives in the first column Laso de la Vega's miracles in the order in which they appear, in the second column the episodes in Sánchez which correspond to them, with their order in Sánchez's work, and in the third column the corresponding episodes in Stradanus, with the numerical order there indicated in parentheses; the order we use is clockwise from the top right, i.e., down the right column and back up the left.

The order, if any, in the correspondences between Laso de la Vega and Stradanus is not immediately apparent. To come to some reasonable hypothesis on the matter, let us assume for the moment that Laso de la Vega as at least director or organizer of the Guadalupe Nahuatl project was basing himself primarily on Sánchez and only thereafter on other sources. In this scenario, he would simply have taken the first six episodes from Sánchez, following the order found there. Unhappy for some reason with Sánchez's seventh miracle, he cast about, still in Sánchez, for another, changing Sánchez's spring description into a miracle. Then he was on his own; he

---

[1]The engraving is discussed in Poole 1995, especially pp. 122–24. A full-page reproduction of it will be found in Peterson 1992.

TABLE 1. INCIDENCE OF MIRACLE STORIES IN THREE SOURCES

Laso de la Vega	*Sánchez*	*Stradanus*
1. arrow wound healed	1.	—
2. epidemic ended	2.	—
3. don Juan de Tovar	3.	—
4. horse accident	4.	(1)
5. lamp falling	5.	(2)
6. candles lit	6.	(4)
7. healing spring	outside the list	—
8. hydropsy, snake	—	—
9. headache	—	(8)
10. Catalina	—	(7)
11. fray Pedro de Villanueva	—	(6)
12. don Luis de Castilla	—	(5)
13. sacristan's child	—	(3)
14. Teotihuacan conflict	—	—

wanted to add more, being more interested in the subject than Sánchez, if only for reasons having to do with his position as vicar in charge of the Guadalupe chapel. His eighth miracle, though in the same vein as the following water cures, is from an unknown source, possibly his own knowledge of local lore; he was surely better placed than most to have picked up anything in the way of oral tradition around the shrine.

From this point on he would have drawn directly on the engraving of Stradanus, either in his possession or coming from his friend Sánchez, who had already used three of its episodes (taken over in turn by Laso de la Vega as his miracles four to six). In Stradanus, the episodes are arranged in two columns on either side of a central image of the Virgin with some text below. As mentioned, the order of Stradanus in Table 1 begins at the top right and proceeds clockwise to the top left. It looks very much as if Sánchez had indeed started at the top right and gone forward selecting in a clockwise fashion, but decided that he preferred number four, the lighting of the candles, to number three, the revival of the sacristan's child (Sánchez includes no individual cures in his selections from Stradanus). Laso de la Vega, seeing the right side apparently already taken, would have started in his continuation at the top left and gone counterclockwise, a procedure just as logical as the opposite. Notice that his numbers nine through twelve correspond to

Stradanus's eight through five in the respective orders. Still hungry for miracles, Laso de la Vega would now have scanned the columns and seen that Sánchez had omitted Stradanus's number three, adding it as his number thirteen. Number fourteen, the Teotihuacan conflict, came from elsewhere; as seen before, the writings of Mendieta are at least one potential source.[2]

Let us survey Laso de la Vega's miracles with the above scenario in mind, seeing if anything about them is explained by their possible sources. Of the first six miracle stories which correspond in Laso de la Vega and Sánchez, we have few clues as to where Sánchez took the first three from;[3] the second three seem to come from Stradanus. In the first episode—the procession, mock skirmish, and arrow wound—Sánchez presents a reasonably full version; in Laso de la Vega the narrative skeleton is the same, but elaborated with detail, some of which is conventional, while some could have been quite easily filled in from general knowledge. Laso de la Vega's account is twice the length of Sánchez's. The narrative method is quite similar to that used in the *Nican mopohua*, except that dialogue is not included. In the second episode, about the epidemic, Laso de la Vega corresponds to Sánchez very closely indeed, with only the addition of a few flowery phrases which do not increase the length of the account by much. In the third story, concerning don Juan of Totoltepec, Laso de la Vega parallels Sánchez almost word for word, merely adding a bit of a speech by the Virgin and an occasional phrase or sentence.

The fourth episode (the story of the runaway horse), and the first of three in which Sánchez was apparently inspired by Stradanus, is already quite well worked up in the *Imagen*, possibly on the basis of development and enlargement of the stories in the public mind in the thirty years since the appearance of the engravings. In Laso de la Vega this episode is extensively reworked, more than any of the other stories. The correspondence as to facts and even wording is again extremely close, but some sentences are arranged in a different sequence, a great deal of description is added, and above all the main character makes a Nahuatl-style speech to his fellows. A good many Nahuatl commonplaces are used in the elaboration, and the character speaks in a polished, idiomatic Nahuatl quite comparable to that used in the speeches of the *Nican mopohua*, although he does not resort to vocatives or

---

[2]See Poole 1995, p. 86.

[3]In the miracle concerning don Juan, Sánchez makes open references (echoed, apparently, in Laso de la Vega) to a published history of the Virgin of Remedios, but given the blatantly pro-Guadalupe tenor of the episode, it is unlikely that the whole account came from any such publication.

polite apologies. The story is much longer in Laso de la Vega than it is in Sánchez.

The fifth story, on the other hand, about the falling lamp, is hardly any longer in Laso de la Vega; it corresponds to Sánchez extemely closely in wording and sequence, down to an apparent Hispanism based on "no solamente . . . sino" and the mysterious phrase "çã çemi," apparently based on Sánchez's "many in one" (see above, p. 13).

The sixth story, about the candles, is again very, very close in the two versions, and actually a bit shorter in Laso de la Vega.

With the seventh item of the miracles, concerning the healing spring, which Laso de la Vega may have taken from a description in Sánchez outside his miracle list, Laso de la Vega is for once a bit less full on the descriptive details than Sánchez. Most of the expansion that occurs starts with Sánchez's statement that the spring is on the spot where the Virgin came to meet Juan Diego when he was trying to avoid her, continuing with a summary of facts from the main apparition account. This part in Laso de la Vega could be seen not as a miracle story per se but as setting the stage for subsequent miracle stories concerning the spring and its waters.

If one surveys the entire set of miracle accounts possibly taken directly from Sánchez, one finds a variety of strategies. Some are expanded, mainly with conventional Nahuatl material, some are left virtually as in Sánchez. One might expect that the adapter or adapters would have done more with the first episodes than with subsequent ones, but such proves not to be strictly the case. Episode four is the most changed and enlarged, with episode one on its heels; episode seven is extensively altered, abbreviated in some ways and expanded in others. Episodes two and three are slightly expanded, and episodes five and six not at all. The difference could apparently be attributed simply to the adapter's taste or to the potential of the individual episodes.

The eighth episode (with hydropsy and the snake), perhaps coming from something Laso de la Vega had heard around the Guadalupe chapel, is fairly extensive, but without the devices of high Nahuatl rhetoric. Episodes nine through thirteen, possibly taken by Laso de la Vega directly from Stradanus, are all short, with no dialogue or other elaboration. An explanation is at hand in the briefness of the captions in Stradanus. In the case of the fourteenth episode, about the sixteenth-century Teotihuacan conflicts, the account is of moderate length and fairly elaborate. The characteristics of the source probably explain its nature, but since we have no indication of the exact origin, little more can be said on the matter.

In brief, it would seem that Laso de la Vega assembled his miracle collection for the first time, using various sources, above all Sánchez and Stradanus, which had a strong impact on the nature of his own accounts. In a few cases he or collaborators assimilated the stories to the general style of the work, but many accounts were left little changed and little elaborated. Note that none of the miracles, with the possible exception of the one at the spring, mentions the apparitions.

The life of Juan Diego at the end of the miracles in Laso de la Vega has little parallel in Miguel Sánchez and is of unknown source. Yet in view of what has already been seen, one must look for every hint of an origin in Sánchez. The *Imagen* (IVM, p. 159; Appx. 2, p. 141) says that Juan Diego requested and received permission from the bishop to serve at the Guadalupe chapel. Several pages later (p. 164) we are told that he died after sixteen years of service, having lived a virtuous, exemplary life. The account in Laso de la Vega could be seen as a bold elaboration of this skeleton in the style of Spanish hagiography. For the most part, Laso de la Vega's account does not contradict Sánchez's framework, merely filling it in in a quite predictable way. There is one difference, however; in Sánchez, Juan Diego leaves his property to all his indigenous neighbors, with religious and philanthropic implications; in Laso de la Vega, he leaves it to his uncle Juan Bernardino, who did not come to live at the chapel.

The remaining larger sections of the *Huei tlamahuiçoltica*, the preface and the *Nican tlantica*, have no relation that is so far apparent to the work of Sánchez; this makes it all the clearer that the apparitions story and miracles are the core of the work, surrounded by introductory and concluding material which are entirely new compositions in a style that combines the Nahuatl sermon and the standard ecclesiastical book introduction. The careful reader keeps coming back to the thought that these parts may have been originally written in Spanish. The final prayer is quite similar, but there was perhaps no need for it to have been composed entirely anew; over the decades ecclesiastics must have had the Salve Regina cast in Nahuatl again and again.

It seems to us that the hypothesis that Laso de la Vega took the core of his book's material from Sánchez, with Stradanus as a second source, is the most likely of the possible explanations of its genesis. Particularly compelling are the facts that formulations in Sánchez often clarify or give a reason for the existence of odd phrases in Laso de la Vega, and that the order of the miracle stories in Laso de la Vega can be put into meaningful relation with the order in both Sánchez and Stradanus. One might object that the translation and adaptation involved in the creation of the Laso de la Vega work could not have been accomplished within the short period of months between the publication of the *Imagen de la Virgen* and that of the *Huei tlamahuiçoltica.*[1] Yet if the additions involved mainly conventional elements and quite mechanical procedures, the task need not have taken very long. Haste could help explain the mistakes found in the work. Above all, although we know the approximate publication dates of both books, we do not know how long the *Imagen* might have lain finished awaiting printing, during which time Laso de la Vega could have acquired a copy from his colleague.

A second possibility is that Laso de la Vega's account preceded Sánchez's and was the source for it. At first glance it might seem that the dependence would be equally likely to go in either direction. Several considerations, however, speak against such a proposition. In his introductory letter to the *Imagen*, Laso de la Vega openly hails Sánchez for having revealed the apparition story to him. The story itself is not of an indigenous type, but is entirely European, following the classic apparition genre of western European pious legends. The Nahuatl of the *Huei tlamahuiçoltica* contains a large number of suspiciously Spanish features, and many of them correspond to things in Sánchez, but there is no hint of Nahuatl syntax, vocabulary, or conventions in the *Imagen*.

A third possibility, that Laso de la Vega and Sánchez were both based on a common source, also encounters obstacles. Any such common source has left no trace whatever. As just seen, Laso de la Vega specifically declared the story new to him. If there was any common source, its wording would have had to have been virtually identical to that of Sánchez at many critical junctures in order to render Laso de la Vega's formulations fully comprehensible. The concatenation of Laso de la Vega, Sánchez, and Stradanus as laid out above virtually precludes the existence of a separate common source, at least for the miracles section.

Nevertheless, we are not dogmatic on these matters. Further study or new discoveries may make things look quite different. We consider our conclusions on the relationship of the *Huei tlamahuiçoltica* and the *Imagen de la Virgen* more as indicated than as definitively established.

The unity of the texts

CONTAINING as they do such disparate matter in apparently divergent styles, the Guadalupe texts give an initial impression of having been written by different people at different times. That the opposite is true cannot per-

---

[1]The letters approving the *Huei tlamahuiçoltica* are dated in January 1649. Laso de la Vega's letter of praise of Sánchez's work in the *Imagen de la Virgen* is dated in July 1648.

haps be definitively proved, but let us approach the question by showing some ways in which it is clear that one writer or team worked on the whole corpus.

The same people must have put the entire body of texts down on paper, and possibly the same person or persons even set them in type. The orthography, the diacritics, the tendencies in spacing (see pp. 32–35) are uniform throughout. Most of the practices were quite widely diffused in the world of ecclesiastical Nahuatl, but some are unusual, and these too are found scattered widely across our texts. The verb *itoa* "to say" has a glottal stop before the *t*. In most ecclesiastical writing of the mid-seventeenth century it would appear as *itoa* or *ìtoa*, but not with a double *tt*, as it and its derivatives predominantly do in the Guadalupe texts, in several different sections. One would think that the additional *t* is a variant representation of the glottal stop, but quite often there is a diacritic on the *i* in addition to the double *tt*: *ìttoa*.[2] Another peculiarity of the Guadalupe corpus is the orthography of derivatives of the word *iiyotl* "breath." In speech, there is a glottal stop between the first *i* and the second one, which is long; thus in ecclesiastical circles the word might be written *ìiyotl* (in Carochi *īyōtl*). Here, however, we frequently find the diacritic on the second *i*, not the first, as *iìyotl*, which if not an out-and-out error is a highly deviant practice; several examples are in the *Nican mopohua*, but one appears in the *Nican motecpana* as well.[3]

Uniformities of the texts go beyond orthographic matters to actual choice of words, meanings, and pronunciations. The most frequent word in the corpus meaning "first" is *yancuican*, which is common and uncontroversial, so that almost anyone writing Nahuatl would have used it, and it tells us little. The other Nahuatl word in this general range varies greatly; *achto* is its most basic but perhaps not most frequent form.[4] The texts use the word only three times, but each time it has the quite rare form *acattopa*, twice in the *Nican mopohua* and once in the *Nican motecpana*. The

---

[2]Examples are in the prefatory section, the *Nican mopohua*, the *Nican motecpana*, and the *Nican tlantica*, pp. 56, 66, 72, 94, 104, 108, 116, 118. The word appears with a more standard orthography on pp. 60, 62, and 74.

[3]Pp. 68, 70, 72, 76, 78, 96. The two *i*'s are also at times written as *i, ì, ii*, and *ìi* (pp. 54, 64, 66, 76, 106, 110, 126).

[4]In a given case the two words can have identical meaning; insofar as they are distinct, *yancuican* points to a thing, person, or event as new in an absolute sense, with no other reference, whereas *achto* makes the phenomenon the first of a potential series. VM, Span./Nahuatl, f. 98v, gives four forms of *achto*, not mentioning *acattopa*. Carochi (AC, f. 98) gives seven forms without mentioning it, but he does then use it in an example.

word *yeppa* is well known in the Nahuatl tradition meaning "previously, always (up to now)"; in the Guadalupe texts it several times has the additional meaning "soon, expectedly" and the like, which as far as we know is not presently attested anywhere else (see p. 43).

The texts are unusual, within the ecclesiastical tradition, in using provincial variants of two particular elements, and furthermore they are somewhat unusual for any Nahuatl writing in going back and forth between the variant and the standard form. In ecclesiastical Nahuatl, and in the language of the Valley of Mexico generally, "much" is *miec*; in the Puebla/Tlaxcala area, many other peripheral regions, and occasionally among (mainly less well educated) writers of the Valley, one finds the older version *miac*. The Guadalupe texts use both, in both the *Nican mopohua* (pp. 66, 72) and the *Nican motecpana* (pp. 92, 94, 96, 102, 104, where *miac* occurs four times, *miec* three, alternating back and forth).[1] Much the same situation obtains with the preterit of the modal auxiliary based on *yauh* "to go", which is -*tia* (*tià*) in the standard Valley of Mexico Nahuatl but -*ta* (-*tà*) in Puebla/Tlaxcala and other peripheral areas, i.e., under much the same conditions in which one would expect *miac* instead of *miec*. Both the *Nican mopohua* (p. 62) and the *Nican motecpana* (pp. 94, 96, 98, 100, 104, 108, 114) use both forms.[2]

Another marked characteristic of the corpus is the presence in all parts of it of some forms that are either true errors or embarrassing slips, mainly of a morphological nature. They are present not only in the portions most likely to have been composed directly by Laso de la Vega, the prefatory matter and the *Nican tlantica*, but in the rest as well, including the *Nican mopohua*. Someone involved in preparing the texts did not grasp the workings of the verb *temachia*, "to trust in, to have hope or confidence in." According to Molina, Carochi, and our own experience of Nahuatl texts, this verb requires an additional object even though its *te-* is by origin the indefinite personal object prefix. Not once in its four appearances in the texts does the verb obey the usual prescription. Twice, once in the *Nican mopohua* (p. 64) and once in the *Nican tlantica* (p. 118), it is treated as intransitive (i.e., with *te-* as sufficient object); twice, in the *Nican tlantica* (pp. 116, 118), it acts as though it must take two objects in addition to *te-*.[3]

---

[1] The *Nican tlantica* has *miec* twice (pp. 70, 72) and no *miac*.

[2] The prefatory section, the *Nican tlantica*, and the final prayer use only -*tia* (pp. 54, 58, 118, 120, 126). The same kind of alternation can occur in the future, but the form occurs in the future only twice in all the texts (pp. 118, 126).

[3] See p. 64, n. 6; p. 116, n. 1; p. 118, n. 1.

Several of the slips have to do with the applicative suffix (usually *-lia*), which, in addition to serving as an applicative or benefactive, functions as part of the reverential formula and can also be absorbed into the main stem of verbs, so that it can appear as many as three times in a single verb complex; it often brings grief to non-native speakers of the language. Forms with a missing or extra *-lia*, or in which a complex with *-lia* could be correct in itself but is shown by the context to have been conceived incorrectly, occur in the prefatory section (p. 56), the *Nican mopohua* (p. 61), the *Nican motecpana* (p. 82), the *Nican tlantica* (pp. 118, 120, 122), and the final prayer (p. 126). An error more of logic than of language appears twice in the texts, consisting of placing a quantifying modifier after, not before, a substantive modifier which really constitutes a unit with the following noun; thus in the *Nican mopohua* we find (p. 80) "Caxtillan nepapan xochitl," "Castile various flowers," instead of the expected "nepapan Caxtillan xochitl," "various Castile flowers" (which in fact occurs on p. 84), and the *Nican motecpana* (p. 96) has "nican omentin tlaca," "here two people," apparently intending "omentin nican tlaca," "two here-people, two local people." The otherwise unattested verb *tlilana*, possibly a mistake for *tlilania* "to trace, write," occurs in the prefatory section (pp. 54, 58) and again in the *Nican tlantica* (p. 116).

A few errors occur in one section only, but are worth specifying to reinforce the general point. In the *Nican mopohua* (p. 73), the form "oquinqualancacuiti," "he made them angry," is erroneous. The mistake might seem trivial, consisting as it does only in the insertion of the two letters *-ca-*, but it is serious in that anyone deeply familiar with Nahuatl realizes that when this kind of element is incorporated into a main verb by means of the preterit "ligature," *-ca* normally has a broadly adverbial sense, whereas here the sense is that of an incorporated object ("to take anger"). In the same section (pp. 66, 86), the optative of the form of purposive motion *-tiuh* is done in a manner going against the prescription of the grammarians.[4] In the *Nican tlantica* (p. 122), "iceltlaçonantzin," intended to mean "his only precious mother," makes a single possessive prefix serve two different purposes in a compound that goes against widely observed practice in Nahuatl texts.[5]

---

[4]The text retains *-tiuh*, whereas Carochi prescribes a glottal stop or *-ti*.

[5]Cases which may be either errors or rare forms are found in the *Nican motecpana* (p. 96; see n. 1) and the *Nican tlantica* (p. 122; see nn. 5, 6).

Loanwords and other language contact phenomena

SPANISH LOANWORDS in the Guadalupe texts fall individually and as a whole into the types characteristic of Stage 2; nowhere are the principal diagnostic signs of Stage 3—loan verbs and particles—to be seen.[1] Although Stage 3 was getting into swing at the time of the book's publication, one is not surprised at this state of things, for the conservative writers of ecclesiastical Nahuatl continued in the main to avoid Stage 3 phenomena far into the eighteenth century. Tables 2 and 3 specify the Spanish words and phrases appearing in the texts, and in which sections they are to be found.

The overall tendency, as in most ecclesiastical writing, is to use loanwords relatively sparingly, with at the same time no hesitation to resort to them when necessary. Even so, the reader may get the impression that loanwords are handled differently in different sections (with possible implications of different authorship). The *Nican mopohua*, especially the story proper, seems to have very few loans indeed, and those of a very basic nature, common in Nahuatl speech at any time from about 1550 forward. In the *Nican motecpana*, on the other hand, loanwords seem more numerous and central to the presentation, and some of them look to be of a type which one would hardly expect before perhaps the last quarter of the sixteenth century (such as *estribo*, "stirrup," or *freno*, "reins"). Indeed, the *Nican mopohua* shows but 12 loanwords, with three more in the image description which is sometimes seen as a part of it, whereas the *Nican motecpana* has 21, and in some of the miracle stories these words are repeated at close intervals. Even so, the difference between 12 and 21 is not overwhelming. If we inspect the *Nican mopohua*, we will sometimes find the word *obispo*, "bishop," repeated at quite close intervals. The invocatory portions of the texts (the preface, the *Nican tlantica*, and the final prayer) have the fewest and most basic loanwords of all.

Another way to approach the matter is to look for clear attempts to avoid loans. If the *Nican motecpana* has the most loans, it also betrays efforts to

---

[1]Stage 1, from Spanish contact to about 1549–1545, involved virtually no borrowing of words from Spanish into Nahuatl; in Stage 2, from then until the mid-seventeenth century, Nahuatl borrowed numerous Spanish nouns but resisted most other kinds of change; in Stage 3, from mid-seventeenth century forward, Nahuatl borrowed also verbs and particles, used calques extensively, made phonological additions from Spanish, and saw other developments related to fairly widespread bilingualism. For a full treatment of the matter see Lockhart 1992, chapter 7.

TABLE 2. LOANWORDS IN THE TEXTS

Word	Translation	in preface	in Nican mopohua	in description	in Nican motecpana	in Nican tlantica	in prayer
aceite	olive oil				*		
altar	altar				*		
ánima	soul				*		*
ángel	angel			*			
caballo	horse				*		
candela	candle				*		
Castilla^a	Castile		*		*		
corona	crown			*			
Cristo	Christ					*	
cruz	cross	*		*			
diciembre	December		*				
Dios	God	*	*		*	*	*
domingo	Sunday		*				
don	Sir, as part of a name		*		*		
español	Spaniard					*	
estribo	stirrup				*		
fray	Friar, as part of a name		*		*		
freno	rein				*		
lámpara	lamp				*		
legua	league (distance)				*		
licenciado	Licentiate, as part of a name				*		
lunes	Monday		*				
martes	Tuesday		*				
mayo	May				*		
misa	mass		*		*		
obispo	bishop		*				
sábado	Saturday		*				
sacristán	sacristan				*		
San, Santa	Saint as part of a name	*	*		*	*	
testamento	testament				*		
vicario	vicar				*		
visorrey	viceroy				*		

^a The word appears exclusively in the normal Nahuatl naturalized form, *Caxtillan*. The text also includes two derived forms: *Caxtiltecatl*, "Spaniard," which is found in the *Nican motecpana* and the *Nican tlantica*, and *Caxtillancayotl*, "something in the Spanish style," in the *Nican mopohua*.

do without them. On p. 104 "a Spanish woman" is rendered with the Stage 1 type phrase "Caxtillan çihuatl," "Castile woman." We have never seen this rare and probably artificial expression before; Nahuatl texts of this time and long before use Spanish *señora* instead. On p. 92 a long circumlocution avoids the use of any words like *cabildo, gobernador, regidores*, or *oficiales de república* in referring to the municipal councils of Mexico City and Tenochtitlan, although such vocabulary had been a staple of Nahuatl texts for many decades. In the *Nican tlantica* (p. 118), the translation "yaotequipanèque" "those performing duty in war" is used instead of the Spanish *soldados*, "soldiers," which by the end of the sixteenth century had become almost as well known a term in Nahuatl as it was in the Spanish of that time.[1] Nothing as contrived occurs in the *Nican mopohua*.

Such expressions smack of Stage 1, but it would be wrong to hasten to attribute the texts themselves, or even the specific usages, to that early period. *Caxtillan* is, it is true, a Stage 1 formation, but it remained in the language for many purposes up to the mid-seventeenth century and long after. Far into Stage 2, a Stage 1 word or phrase might be paired with a Spanish loan by way of clarification, becoming part of a frozen expression that could be retained even on into Stage 3 (as *noyolia nanima* "my means of living, my soul" was in the Coyoacan region).[2] Such is the nature of the frequently used pair *teopixcatlatoani obispo*, "priestly ruler, bishop," in the *Nican mopohua*. It often happens in the languages of the world that archaic forms acquire an elegant tone; the same thing was happening in Nahuatl, and in ecclesiastical Nahuatl in particular. When "quauhnepanoltitech" "on the joined wood (i.e., the cross)" is used in the preface (p. 56), it is not merely to avoid *cruz*, which also appears in this section, but for stylistic variation and added elegance.[3]

Spanish loan phrases in the texts are much like the loanwords proper,

---

[1]The phrase "huei Acalli," "big boat," (p. 120) could be seen as an artificial attempt to avoid Spanish *navío* "ship", but Chimalpahin's writings give evidence that the word was quite unfamiliar to him as well, so that he too sometimes said *acalli* or accompanied the Spanish word with that explanation (Lockhart 1992, pp. 292, 564 n. 72). On pp. 116–18, "motepozpachoz" for "it will be printed" is rather recherché, but some *tepoz-* compound was doubtless called for (VM has *tepoztlacuiloa*), since a loan verb such as *imprimiroa* would clearly be out of place in a normal ecclesiastical text (and that verb has not yet been attested in any case).

[2]Ongoing work of Rebecca Horn and Doris Namala with eighteenth-century Coyoacan testaments.

[3]The use of *nican tlaca* "here people, indigenous people" (see pp. 37–39 below) has the same aura.

TABLE 3. LOAN PHRASES, SAINTS' NAMES

Word or phrase	Translation	in preface	in Nican mopohua	in descrip- tion	in Nican motecpana	in Nican tlantica	in prayer
altar mayor	main altar				*		
Audiencia Real	Royal High Court				*		
Espíritu Santo	Holy Spirit	*					*
San Bue- naventura	St. Bona- venture	*					
Jesu Cristo	Jesus Christ		*			*	*
Jesús	Jesus						*
media legua	half a league				*		
mil y qui- nientos y treinta y uno	1531 (and 1544, 1548, 1563 in same style)		*		*		
mil y qui- nientos y quarenta y cuatro años	year of 1544				*		
Nueva España	New Spain		*			*	
Remedios	[Virgin of] Remedies				*		
San Agustín	St. Augustine				*	*	
San Fran- cisco	St. Francis		*		*	*	
santa iglesia	holy church				*		
Santa María	St. Mary			*	*	*	
Santa María de Guadalupe	St. Mary of Guada- lupe				*		

nothing exceptional for the time of publication or long before. The *Nican motecpana* has the largest number of them, predominating even more than in the matter of loanwords, primarily because there is more occasion to name saints and church appurtenances in that section. Here too appears the phrase *media legua*, "half a league," the most daring of the lot because of its incorporation of a quantitative adjective, but such things are seen in mundane texts of the time as well. The most obvious explanation of the use of the phrase is that it occurs also in the version of this particular miracle to be found in the work of Sánchez, Laso de la Vega's probable source.

Generally speaking, the phrases are just as they would be in any other kind of Nahuatl text, but there is one exception. In giving a year, lay Spaniards often duplicated the word *año*: "en el año de mil y . . . años." Nahuatl texts generally followed suit, sometimes entirely in Spanish, sometimes with the first *año* replaced by *xihuitl*, the Nahuatl equivalent. In the Guadalupe texts, a ratiocinative ecclesiastical mind has been at work attempting to purify or correct this convention. *Xihuitl* is used in all cases, a normal feature, but not once in the several such phrases is it followed by the usual *de*. Even more striking, and in the face of normal Nahuatl usage, is the general omission of *años* at the end of the phrase, in both the *Nican mopohua* and the *Nican motecpana*. Once, however (p. 114), the *Nican motecpana* falls back into giving the conventional final word: "xihuitl mil y quinientos y quarenta y quatro años."

Over and above the matter of loanwords or substitutes for loans in a text, one needs to consider the presence or absence of whole phrases using Nahuatl vocabulary but influenced by Spanish. The elaborate frozen calques, usually with a verb or particle equivalence at the core, which were so characteristic of Stage 3 Nahuatl are missing. A beginning in that direction can be detected, the use of the verb *pia*, originally "to guard, keep, control," as an equivalent of Spanish *tener* "to have" in various common idioms. In the image description (p. 88), *pia* like *tener* is used to indicate an object's measurements; in the *Nican motecpana* it appears in the sense "to have" a child (p. 110) and to indicate age (p. 114). These usages, however, are well attested in mundane Nahuatl documents of the late sixteenth and early seventeenth centuries, forming at most a gradual approach to the explosion of such expressions in Stage 3.[1]

The *pia* idioms had become well established in Nahuatl by Laso de la

---

[1] It is interesting that *pia* idioms are in general more characteristic of mundane than of ecclesiastical Nahuatl. Another possible but dubious case of Spanish influence on a verb in the texts is the use of *polihui* (p. 120), usually "to disappear, be destroyed, etc.," in the meaning "to be absent, missing," like Spanish *faltar*. *Polihui* does seem eventually to have entered into an equivalence relationship with *faltar*. It remains entirely possible, however, that the "be absent" meaning had developed even before the Spanish advent. Molina, who fails to reflect even the *pia* equivalence, gives this sense of *polihui* in one of his glosses (VM, Span./Nahuatl, f. 62).

Vega's time. What is more striking in the Guadalupe texts is the presence of Spanish-influenced expressions which were *not* normal Nahuatl usage. The most flagrant examples are to be found in the invocatory material, as one might expect, but they occur throughout. In Nahuatl generally, mass was seen (using *itta*), not heard (which would involve the verb *caqui*) as in Spanish. Yet the *Nican mopohua* (p. 70) has "omocac Missa," "mass was heard." In the *Nican motecpana* (p. 112) one finds the rare phrase *quiximati cihuatl* ("aic quiximà çihuatl," "he never knew a woman, was without sexual experience"), resting on an idiom common in ecclesiastical Spanish and going ultimately back to the Hebrew. Louise Burkhart has brought to our attention that the expression is found in some other ecclesiastical texts.

A subtle example of possible Spanish-derived phraseology is the case of the construction *amo çaniyo . . . no ihuan*, "not only . . . but also." The phrase does occur in texts by native speakers and must be considered at some level idiomatic Nahuatl. At the same time, it is quite rare. In the Guadalupe texts it is used several times (pp. 72–74, 92, 102, 122) in a way that makes one think of the similar Spanish *no sólo* (or *solamente*). . . *sino*. In two cases, one in the *Nican mopohua* (pp. 72–74) and the other in the miracles (p. 102), the Spanish phrase is actually found at the corresponding spot in Sánchez's book, strongly suggesting, though surely not proving, Laso de la Vega's dependence on Sánchez.

One of the most foreign-sounding passages in the entire corpus occurs in Laso de la Vega's preface (p. 54): "izçenca ic òpoliuhca in cahuitl in iuh-catiliz," "which had disappeared through the nature of time." *Cahuitl* is doubtless the closest Nahuatl approximation to the word "time"; in Nahuatl usage, however, it is practically never seen in the pure abstract sense, but with some modifier (as in the common *ixquich cahuitl*, "the whole time, as long as, until"). When one adds the rare and abstract word *iuhcatiliztli*, "form or nature of something," the effect is highly unusual. It is heightened by the use of the pluperfect (an extremely rare tense in Nahuatl) of the verb *polihui*.[2] One can hardly avoid the impression that the passage is a translation of a Spanish phrase such as "que por la constitución del tiempo había desaparecido," already written down on paper or existing in the mind of the author. This passage has its parallels in the *Nican tlantica* (p. 116), where *cahuitl* is twice used in the same way. The effect is exacerbated by

---

[2]The pluperfect also appears four times in the *Nican tlantica* (pp. 116, 120, 122). Each case can be accepted as correct, even in a sense idiomatic, but overall one gets the feeling of a person thinking in Spanish and translating into Nahuatl.

the fact that as the subject of a verb, *cahuitl* becomes an active agent: "in oquipolò in cahuitl," "which time destroyed"; "quipòpoloz in cahuitl," "time will destroy it."[1]

Diacritics, orthography, and spacing

FROM THE mid-seventeenth century or somewhat earlier, ecclesiastical publications in Nahuatl tended to indicate glottal stop but not (with the notable exception of Carochi's grammar) vowel length. The principal marking device was the grave accent, not the *h* which was used in ecclesiastical texts in the sixteenth century, and also in documents by native Nahuatl speakers for as long as production continued.[2] Marking was highly erratic, ignoring a large number of glottal stops in all positions, but above all word-finally (as in mundane Nahuatl texts too).

The present text falls into the general late ecclesiastical tradition. By far the most common diacritic is the grave accent. In the great majority of cases, it appears on a vowel followed by a glottal stop; in most of the others it indicates the masculine vocative *-e*.[3] A few times it falls on a vowel, sometimes long, sometimes short, that is not accompanied by glot-

---

[1] Among the signs of a new kind of Spanish influence on Nahuatl from mid-seventeenth century forward was the increased marking of plurals of inanimates. The presence of such plurals would by no means necessarily point to the participation of a Spaniard, since the new-style plural marking penetrated deeply into ordinary Nahuatl usage. But in any case, plurals are mainly handled conservatively in the Guadalupe texts. For example, the flowers Juan Diego saw and picked are consistently treated as grammatically singular (pp. 78–80). One even finds a nicely calibrated usage like that of the sixteenth century in "inic tlatlaz candelas," "for the candles to burn" (p. 102), where the verb "tlatlaz," having an inanimate subject, is singular, although the Spanish loanword "candelas" bears a plural as it would in the language from which it came. The construction "xiuhtotontin," "weeds or little grasses," has an overt plural despite being inanimate (pp. 64, 78), but from an early time plurals with the *-ton* diminutive often bore a nominal plural ending, as though *-ton* were itself an animate noun. The stars in the Virgin's costume once appear marked plural ("çiçitlaltin," p. 90), but the old grammars tell us that as apparently animate beings stars had always received such marking. The only true and unexplainable inanimate plural in the corpus refers to the rays surrounding the Virgin's head ("màtlactin omome," "twelve," p. 90). Thus the texts are well within the usage of their time as to plural marking, and we can deduce little about likely authorship or time of composition from the matter. One can say, however, that plurals are handled in the same manner throughout the whole book.

[2] This *h* does appear once, in the word "çemihcac," "eternal," in the heading of the preface (p. 52).

tal stop. The instances being relatively few, we have indicated each one in the notes. The student of Nahuatl can thus trust that with the others, except for the quite obvious vocatives, the glottal stop, which after all is a consonant of the language as important as any, is indeed present. The lack of an accent, however, does not imply the absence of glottal stop. As expected, the accent is quite rare on a word-final vowel, and the diacritic may be omitted at any point. Only perhaps three-fourths even of word-internal glottal stops are marked. Common words vary back and forth constantly, for example between "teòcalli," "temple, church," and "teocalli," or "tzàtzi," "to cry out," and "tzatzi."

In thirty-plus cases, the text indicates final glottal stop despite the general tendency not to. Most of these are stem-internal, mainly the preterits of Class 3 verbs (ending therefore in *-i* or *-ò*, as with "onimitznahuatì," "I ordered you," and "oticmahuiçò," "you beheld it," on p. 80). A very few, not more than three or four, are present-tense plurals, like "conì," "they drink it," on p. 104, and an equal number are preterit plurals, like "onquizquè," "they came out," on p. 98. The text betrays a strong reluctance to indicate glottal stops in two consecutive syllables, and in fact, immediately consecutive glottals are nowhere marked.[4] The stem *tlatoca-*, repeatedly used in the text's equivalents for "queen," contains two glottal stops, one after the first *a* and another after the *o*. In any given case only one or the other is shown; thus p. 94 has "toçihuapillatòcatzin" and p. 96 "toçihuapillàtocatzin," "our queen."[5]

A very secondary diacritic in the text is the circumflex, appearing by our count a total of 33 times. Here the clarity of intention that is so easy to discern with the grave accent is lacking. The sign is applied once to an *a* followed by glottal stop ("tehuellâmachti," "pleasing," on pp. 60–62). The five circumflexes on *o* are all on a long vowel unassociated with glottal stop; in fact, all these cases involve the preterit *o*. The rest of the circum-

---

[3]In a single exceptional passage, the same just referred to in n. 2, p. 28, the acute accent is used instead, for glottal stop ("tlatócaçihuapille," "O Queen") as well as for the vocative ("ichpochtzintlé," "O Virgin"). In the Spanish sections at the beginning of the book, the grave accent indicates stress, and is also used with the preposition *a*, "to," differentiating it from *a* (*ha*), the third person singular of the verb *haber*.

[4]One case looks close: "quihualtzìtzitzquìtiàque," "they came holding her" (p. 108). But in fact the syllable *ti* stands between the two marked vowels.

[5]A similar set occurs on p. 90 in relation to the modal auxiliary *-ticac*, which has a glottal stop after the *i*, and a main verb whose stem ends in glottal stop: "quimoyahualhuìticac" and "quimoyahualhuitìcac," "it surrounds it."

flex accents appear on *i*, long about as often as short, with a few dubious cases, and one in which the diacritic replaces an *n* or *m* after short *i*. Given such small certainty about the intention of the marking, we have not made any indication in the notes about the situation as to glottal stop or vowel length in the various instances.

A diacritic of a different order is the one found on vowels scattered through the text, indicating a following nasal consonant, *n* or *m*.[1] This mark was not invented for Nahuatl but was a standard part of Spanish calligraphy and printing. In some hands, there is a clear distinction between a primarily horizontal (in practice often curved) overbar over vowels to indicate following nasals and the twisted tilde over an *n* (*ñ*) to indicate its palatalization; in other hands no such distinction can be detected, the different contexts alone indicating the intention. Printers often used the tilde for both purposes. We were at first inclined to take the marks in the printed Nahuatl text here as overbars. Many, however, are clearly tildes. With some others, clarity is not to be attained directly, but the marks are identical to ones in Spanish sections of the book which can only mean tilde. Thus we eventually decided to reproduce all the signs as tilde, to be interpreted according to the context. In many cases here, as in its handling generally, the tilde/overbar is used to shorten a line when space is needed. In other places, it may be ornamental, or may have served to relieve the typesetter of tedium. It is possible that the overbar took such a hold in Nahuatl calligraphy, often far exceeding what is usually seen in Spanish documents, because of the notable weakness of syllable-final nasals in Nahuatl pronunciation.

Spelling. In other aspects of orthography, the text falls within the ordinary range for ecclesiastical writings of the time and is particularly close to the tradition best embodied in Carochi's *Arte*. The two agree in rendering syllable-final [k^W] as -*uc* (as in "Teteuctin," "lords," on p. 88), *iya* as *ia* (for example, "pohuia," "belonged," on p. 60),[2] and *n* before an [s] sound as *z*, recognizing the assimilation in speech, above all when the particle *in* is

---

[1]The sign occurs constantly over *a*, quite rarely over *e* and *o* (eight times each), and not at all over *i*, possibly for typographical reasons.

[2]Both in Carochi and here, *iyo* is written out in full. See, however, "iquezquilhuioc," "a few days [into December]," p. 60; "momachioti" and "omomachiotìtzino," "it imprinted itself," on pp. 60, 62; and "in itlallo, in içoquio," "his earthly body," on p. 98. There are also inconsistencies with *ia* for *iya*, mainly involving the retention of a root-initial *y* when a prefix ending in *i* precedes, as in "niyauh," "I am going"; more serious is an example such as "quiyahuac," "outside" (p. 122) ("quiahuac" also occurs, p. 106).

involved (as in "izçihuapilli," "the Lady," on p. 74).[3] Like Carochi, and most mundane documents for that matter, the text does not usually assimilate an *n* to a following *m*. A major feature of both is the tendency to write *i* for syllabic [i] in all cases, leaving *y* for the glide only (as in *ye*, "already"), whereas mundane Nahuatl texts, following secular Spanish practice, tended to spell the first [i] in a word or tight phrase as *y*, restricting *i* to internal use.

Adherence to the Carochi norm is not, however, complete. In general, the text tends, although with numerous exceptions, to put a cedilla on all *c*'s pronounced as [s], including those before *e* and *i*; the practice was common enough, if by mid-seventeenth century a bit old fashioned, both among mundane writers and in ecclesiastical circles. Although initial syllabic *i* is dominant as in Carochi's canon, an undercurrent of *y* can be discerned. The related set of words *iuh, iuhqui, iuhquin*, occurring over ninety times, with a range of meanings such as "thus, as, like, seemingly" is mainly written with initial *y* throughout the text. *Ihuan*, "and," frequently appears as *yhuan*. The particle *in* is seen several times as *yn*, all except one case falling in the first pages of the *Nican mopohua*.[4] Sometimes *hu* is written where the glide is not an inherent part of the word, especially in *tlatoani*, "ruler," which always appears as "tlàtohuani" or "tlatohuani."[5] It is tempting to think that these traits, especially the initial *y*'s in the first part of the *Nican mopohua*, are relics of texts first written in the mundane Nahuatl tradition, then recopied in a different orthography by Laso de la Vega and/or an amanuensis, with some slips.[6] Yet the same general characteristics obtain not only in the *Nican mopohua* and the *Nican motecpana*, but in the portions most clearly written from scratch for the book, the preface and the *Nican tlantica*. An amanuensis, though trained in the churchly tradition, would

---

[3]In the Guadalupe texts, as with Carochi, the assimilation occurs only within a phonological phrase, between a particle and a following particle or nuclear word. Here, overwhelmingly only the particle *in* is assimilated to a following [s] (all other cases amount to only five). Even this restricted practice is not carried out with full consistency; see "in çenca," "the very" (p. 54, also several other times), or "in çenquizcaichpochtli," "the consummate Virgin," (p. 60).

[4]Actually, the same tendencies can be observed in Carochi's *Arte*, although far less pronounced.

[5]The *h* for glottal stop referred to in n. 2, p. 28, would be a similar phenomenon, that is, something by that time more common in documents done independently by Nahuatl speakers than in ecclesiastical texts.

[6]Such appears to be the origin of some initial *y* and *h* for glottal stop in the Carochi-sponsored text of the Bancroft Dialogues. See ANS, p. 97.

inevitably have known the mundane tradition as well, and he could have slipped into it inadvertently. And indeed, Laso de la Vega himself must have been exposed to mundane Nahuatl writing and older ecclesiastical productions, and as a result he conceivably had a soft spot in his heart for initial *y* and other features frowned on by the Jesuits, as some of us still do today.

In handwritten Nahuatl documents of the sixteenth and seventeenth centuries (as in comparable Spanish texts) there is often no clear distinction between upper and lower case. In a printed book there is, and capital letters are used here in a quite significant and consistent fashion. Nearly all utterances beginning after a period have an initial capital letter. Proper names are almost always capitalized, and beyond that, capitalization is applied selectively to certain words or roots, especially the names and titles of the Virgin, often clearly as an indication of importance or respect, but sometimes for obscure reasons.

Spacing and punctuation. Modern grammarians and philologists of Nahuatl have properly insisted on the necessity of a particular kind of word division, writing each noun or verb with its prefixes and suffixes as a separate entity marked by a space on each side, and the same with particles, even the smallest, such as *in* and *oc*. Sixteenth- and seventeenth-century writers of Nahuatl proceeded quite differently. Generally they tended to write a unit larger than the modern "word" solid, and they often put particles together with the following nuclear word; hardly anyone wrote the ubiquitous particle *in* separate from what followed. No writer, mundane or ecclesiastical, was ever entirely consistent, but the spectrum was wide, from a practice in the Sahagún corpus that approaches the modern, to total lack of attention to spacing in some mundane texts (as in most secular Spanish texts of the time, as far as that goes). Indeed, for Nahuatl at least, the "space," with all the implications we attach to it today, did not yet exist.[1]

The Guadalupe text, as printed, falls into the normal range as to spacing, closer perhaps to the mundane tradition than to Sahagún and Carochi, with some peculiarities. Whatever the inconsistencies, spacing appears to be taken seriously. When a string of letters, although it may seem to us an arbitrary or miscellaneous agglomeration, must be broken at the end of a line, a hyphen indicates the unity of the string; even Sahagún's copyists did not go so far, making no distinction between a broken string and one which simply ended with the line. The observer must wonder why so much care was exercised, for the spacing falls far short of following consistent princi-

---

[1]Compare Lockhart 1993, p. 26, and Lockhart 1995, pp. 134–35.

ples. It is not, however, entirely chaotic. Never are two consecutive nuclear words written without an intervening space. Sizable particles are usually written separately too. A space never splits a minimal morpheme. The article *in* is mainly included in the following string.

The principal variation occurs within the nuclear phrase. A verb complex may be written solid, or a space may be inserted between the prefixes and the stem, as in "quinmo manahuiliaya," "she defended them," or between one or two initial prefixes and all the rest, as in "quin mocuitlahuìtzinozque," "they should care for them." With nouns, the possessive prefix may be included in the unit, the normal procedure today, or the article and the prefix may be written separately, as in "inin netolinilizpan," "in their afflictions." Compound nouns and verbs may appear as a unit or may be divided between major constituents, as in "initlaçò ixiptlatzin," "her precious image." Somewhat the same awareness of constituents within complexes is shown by the occasional capitalization of the main root, as in "totlaçòmahuizNantzin," "our precious revered mother."

Punctuation may follow immediately upon the preceding letters, the present-day convention, or it may have a space on each side; the same wavering is seen in many books of the time, including Carochi's nearly contemporaneous *Arte*. The punctuation itself is that of the age, and, as in most ecclesiastical Nahuatl texts, is laid on generously (unlike texts in the mundane Nahuatl tradition, where it is often virtually absent). The period approaches present-day norms in its use, but the distinction between comma, semicolon, and colon is vaguer. Semicolon and colon are nearly identical, usually separating major clauses; they often precede *auh* (indication of preceding full stop) or words introducing independent clauses like *ihuan*, "and," and *niman ic*, "thereupon." The comma, by far the most common punctuation mark, above all delineates parallel words and phrases and introduces clearly dependent clauses, but it also overlaps with the semicolon and colon, and it can be found before *auh*.

The original recognizes paragraphs, sometimes by beginning with all capital letters, sometimes by indentation. In some sections, and particularly in the *Nican mopohua*, the paragraph units nearly take on the proportions of chapters. For ease in reading and also in order to keep the corresponding parts of the Nahuatl and English more closely aligned, we have created new paragraphs. We have also highlighted longer speeches by indenting them throughout, a feature not present in the original publication. The reader can still detect the original paragraphing, because in our translation original paragraphs begin with a few words in small capitals, unindented, whereas the new ones begin in lower case, with indentation. The Nahuatl transcription makes the same distinction in a different way, so that we could avoid adding capitals to those already there, for doing so would mean either changing some *u*'s to *V* to obey the universal convention of that time, or violating that convention with a capital *U*.[1] The original's paragraphs, which as mentioned sometimes begin with capitals and no indentation, sometimes with indentation and no capitals, are preserved just as they were. Our new paragraphs in the Nahuatl have neither capitals nor indentation.

In our transcription we have retained all letters, diacritics, capitalization, and punctuation marks exactly as in the original, but we have spaced everything according to present-day norms, with particles, verb complexes, and noun complexes as separate units except where they are orthographically assimilated to one another, and with all punctuation attached to the word immediately preceding. Although the original spacing is not without interest, reproducing it would greatly impede the understanding of the text for all but the very most expert readers. To give a sense of the original and how we have proceeded, we include here a section (HT, ff. 14–14v; below, pp. 110–12) with both the original spacing and our alteration of it.

Original	Our version
YN oc itzinècan, in oc ipeuhyan inì-	YN oc itzinècan, in oc ipeuhyan in
quac monexîti ini tlaçò ixiptlatzin	ìquac monexîti in itlaçòixiptlatzin
izçenquizca ichpochtzintli Totlaçò-	izçenquizcaichpochtzintli Totlaçò-
nantzin Guadalupe in nican tlaca tlà-	nantzin Guadalupe in nican tlaca
toque Pipiltin huel itechtzinco mo-	tlàtoque Pipiltin huel itechtzinco
tzatziliaya inic quinmopalehuiliaya ,	motzatziliaya inic quinmopalehui-
inic quinmo manahuiliaya inin neto-	liaya, inic quinmomanahuiliaya in
linilizpan, ihuan inin miquiztem-	innetolinilizpan, ihuan in inmiquiz-
pan, içen mactzinco mo cahuaya	tempan, içenmactzinco mocahuaya
çemè yèhuan in, intlàtohuani catca	çemè yèhuan in, in tlàtohuani catca
Dõ Francisco Quetzlalmamalitzin	Dõ Francisco Quetzlalmamalitzin
Teotihuàcan inìquac xixin in altepetl	Teotihuàcan in ìquac xixin in alte-
in huel cactimoman, inniman aocac	petl in huel cactimoman, in niman
mocauhtiquiz inic àmo quinmoca-	aocac mocauhtiquiz inic àmo quin-
hualiz tlamachiltiaya in San Fran-	mocahualiztlamachiltiaya in San
cisco Teopixque, inquinequia Tlà-	Francisco Teopixque, in quinequia

---

[1]Whenever we repeat in lower case something given in caps in the original, we naturally change the *v* back to *u*, as in *Nican mopohua*, not *Nican mopohva*, which was not the intention and which is very painful to the experienced eye.

tohuani Visorrey Don Luys de Velasco yèhuantzitzin in San Augustin Teopixque quin mocuitlahuìtzinozque, huel ic cenca netoliniliztli quittaque in altepehuàque. Auh inin tlàtocauh Don Francisco, ihuan ini piloan ça motlàtlatitinemia, yè ica huel nohuian temoloya; auh oncan hualla izça tlaçaccan in Azcapotzalco, auh ichtaca quihualmotlatlauhtiliaya in ilhuicac Çihuapilli Guadalupe maquimoyollotili ini tlaçòconetzin in Visorrey, ihuan in tlàtoque Audiencia Real inic tlapòpolhuililozq̃ altepehuàque inic huelmocuepazque in inchan, ihuan ocçeppa macozque in San Francisco Teopixque, auh huel yuhmochiuh, ca otlapòpolhuililoque in altepehuàque, ihuan in intlatòcauh inin pillohuan , ihuan ocçeppa macoque in San Francisco Teopixque, inic quinmocuitlahuizque, ihuan mochintin hualmocuepque inin chan aocmo mà ic toliniloque: mochiuh ye ipan xihuitl mil y quinientos y cincuenta y ocho, no ihuan inye imiquiztempan in Dõ Francisco huel içenmactzinco mocauh inilhuicac Çihuapilli Totlaçònantzin Guadalupe inic ipan motlàtoltiz ini yolia, ini anima, auh mohuenchiuhta inixpantzinco, iniuh neztica inipã itestamento in huel tlayacatitica itlàtol, itlatecpan, mochiuh ic omilhuitl mani Março inipan xihuitl mil y quinientos y sesenta y tres.

Tlàtohuani Visorrey Don Luys de Velasco yèhuantzitzin in San Augustin Teopixque quinmocuitlahuìtzinozque, huel ic cenca netoliniliztli quittaque in altepehuàque. Auh in intlàtocauh Don Francisco, ihuan in ipiloan ça motlàtlatitinemia, yèica huel nohuian temoloya; auh oncan hualla izça tlaçaccan in Azcapotzalco, auh ichtaca quihualmotlatlauhtiliaya in ilhuicac Çihuapilli Guadalupe ma quimoyollotili in itlaçòconetzin in Visorrey, ihuan in tlàtoque Audiencia Real inic tlapòpolhuililozq̃ altepehuàque inic huel mocuepazque in inchan, ihuan oc çeppa macozque in San Francisco Teopixque, auh huel yuh mochiuh, ca otlapòpolhuililoque in altepehuàque, ihuan in intlatòcauh in inpillohuan, ihuan oc çeppa macoque in San Francisco Teopixque, inic quinmocuitlahuizque, ihuan mochintin hualmocuepque in inchan aocmo mà ic toliniloque: mochiuh ye ipan xihuitl mil y quinientos y cincuenta y ocho, no ihuan in ye imiquiztempan in Dõ Francisco huel içenmactzinco mocauh in ilhuicac Çihuapilli Totlaçònantzin Guadalupe inic ipan motlàtoltiz in iyolia, in ianima, auh mohuenchiuhta in ixpantzinco, in iuh neztica in ipã itestamento in huel tlayacatitica itlàtol, itlatecpan, mochiuh ic omilhuitl mani Março in ipan xihuitl mil y quinientos y sesenta y tres.

Aspects of usage in the texts

Altepetl. Much of the progress of recent Nahuatl studies has had to do with a recognition of the nature and centrality of the altepetl, the local ethnic state which was the master entity of Nahua sociopolitical and even cultural life. In a text concerning an extra-altepetl phenomenon, the macro-regional saint Guadalupe, and whose composition was directed if not out-and-out performed by a Spanish priest, we have little reason to expect either that the term will be prominent or that it will be well understood (it seems, for example, to have largely escaped Sahagún). The word is indeed not prominent in the Laso de la Vega texts, and it shows certain peculiarities, but it does after all follow the main lines of Nahuatl usage.

A characteristic Nahua mode was to imagine the totality of the people of a region or of the world as a collection of altepetl units and to speak of them in those terms. The Guadalupe texts reflect this usage perfectly. When everyone began coming to see the image at the Mexico City cathedral, the passage (p. 88) starts "huel çenmochi izçemaltepetl olin," "there was a movement in all the altepetls." And again, with the first procession to the shrine (p. 92), the text mentions the Mexica nobles "ihuan in oc çequin nohuian altepehuàcan tlaca," "as well as the people from other altepetls all around." The Nahua altepetl had borders and lands and hence a geographical dimension, but it was above all a certain kind of organization of people. Thus the text is in the mainstream of Nahuatl usage when it says (p. 110) that at the time of troubles in Teotihuacan over which religious order should administer the church, "xixin in altepetl," "the altepetl dispersed."

Nearly half of the occurrences of the word "altepetl" in the text concern Mexico City: not the indigenous altepetl of Tenochtitlan in its surviving form, but the Spanish city. These instances are probably best seen as a Nahuatl translation of "Ciudad de México." In that case it would be easier to appreciate the rather unusual geographic specificity of the expression (p. 66) "in oàcico ìtic altepetl," "when he got inside the altepetl," with its impression of arriving inside the built-up part of the city proper. In texts written by Nahuas, the distinction between the more urban and more rural part of the altepetl was very rarely made. Mexico City is, it is true, a special case in that even in preconquest times the territory of the altepetl hardly exceeded the more or less urban entity surrounded by the lake.

Although we have attempted to cast our translation in easily under-standable language with few special or foreign terms, we have retained the Nahuatl word "altepetl" in the English. Such is the growing tendency in Nahuatl philology, and for good reason. Not only is there no good English equivalent, but it is important to highlight the occurrences of the term if we are to gain a yet fuller understanding of its important place in Nahua thought and language. In Nahuatl, the word usually has no overt plural except when it refers specifically to the people of the entity, and this use of the singular for the plural as well is often carried over into English. We sympathize, but in the present case we have adopted the perhaps somewhat inelegant but clear plural form "altepetls."

"Indian" equivalents. By the time of Stage 2, postconquest Nahuatl was receptive to Spanish loans in general and to the loan of Spanish ethnic terminology in particular, yet it made very little use indeed of the ubiquitous Spanish word *indio*, "Indian." Two terms served as close referential equivalents, though with different connotations than the Spanish word. *Nican tlacatl*, "here person," "local person," with its occasional variant *iz tlacatl*,[1] came to prominence first, continuing in use through most of the sixteenth century. From very early, however, another word, *macehualli*, "commoner," gravitated in the same direction, and by about 1600 it had become predominant, with *nican tlacatl* fading out. *Macehualli* had originally meant something like "human being, ordinary person," and its plural *macehualtin* still often had the effect of "the people," so the new sense required no large semantic stretch. The plural was by far the more common form, most of the time with a mock-reverential ending indicating, in this context, humility: *macehualtzitzintin*.[2]

The Guadalupe texts, despite their constant mention of native people and their closeness to the work of Sánchez, in which the word *indio* is sprinkled liberally over the pages, follow Nahuatl usage of the time closely; the Spanish word never appears in the Nahuatl portions. *Macehualtzitzintin* is, as one would expect, the most frequent form. Some of the subtleties of Nahuatl usage are well reflected. In Nahuatl, most of the time the word could be given the interpretation "commoner" as well as "indigenous person." Thus when Juan Diego is introduced (p. 60) as a "maçehualtzintli," we can take it that he is a poor commoner or an "Indian," or both; he is both in fact. Similar usage can be found in the voluminous writings of Chimalpahin.

The possessed form of *macehualli* was employed in a meaning very distinct from that of the absolutive in the Nahuatl of the sixteenth and seventeenth centuries, meaning "subject" or "vassal" regardless of rank or

---

[1]*Nican* and *iz* both mean "here," but *iz* is seen mainly only in certain frozen expressions such as *iz catqui*, "here is."

[2]See Lockhart 1992, pp. 114–16.

ethnicity. When this form of the word is used with Juan Diego and Juan Bernardino, referring to them in relation to the Virgin (pp. 66, 76), we cannot be sure, perhaps, just what is intended (i.e., "vassal" or "indigenous person"), but when Laso de la Vega applies it to himself (p. 58), we know that the text is using the possessed form in the standard Nahuatl fashion.

Further nuances are to be observed. Hints of the old meaning "people" without much additional connotation occur in both the *Nican mopohua* and the *Nican motecpana* (pp. 72, 92); in both cases the form is "maçehualli," without the mock reverential and using the singular as a collective. In two cases, one in the description of the image and one in the *Nican tlantica* (pp. 88, 122), "maçehualtzitzintin" specifically means commoners as opposed to nobles; both references are to earlier times.

All of these usages are clearly within the normal practice of Nahuatl in the first half of the seventeenth century. About another subtlety of usage in the text we are not so sure. In texts written by Nahuas, one can find instances in which the people referred to as *macehualtzitzintin* include, by implication, nobles as well as commoners, but at present we know of no text in which a noble or prominent person is specifically so denominated. The Guadalupe texts, in the *Nican tlantica*, do use the word this way, calling the noble don Juan de Tovar a "maçehualtzintli" (p. 118), and again referring to him and Juan Diego as two "maçehualtzitzintin" (p. 120). It is quite possible, even probable, that usage among Nahuas eventually reached this point, but it is also possible that these passages reflect Spanish influence. That is, Laso de la Vega, with the Sánchez text in his mind, may have used the word in these cases as an outright equivalent of Spanish *indio*, which it never quite became in Nahuatl as generally spoken.

The phrase that was first predominant among Nahuas for indigenous people, *nican tlacatl*, also appears in the Guadalupe texts. It occurs in all the major sections except the *Nican mopohua* itself,[1] always in the plural (*nican tlaca*), referring to local people as a group or in general. Its use corresponds to what is seen in texts written by Nahuas except for the timing, for generally speaking it had faded out by the time the Guadalupe texts were published. Many instances can be found in the work of Chimalpahin (who wrote mainly in the time 1600–1625), but on close inspection one sees that most or all must originate in older texts which Chimalpahin copied. It is tempting, then, to try to detect earlier portions of the Guadalupe texts by the presence of the earlier term. Thus one might think that the first miracles listed in the *Nican motecpana*, which indeed deal with an earlier time than

---

[1]Also not in the brief final prayer.

most, and two of which use the term *nican tlacatl*, rest on some form of Nahuatl text much older than the models for those that follow. In fact, however, the expression appears also in the sections most clearly composed entirely new by Laso de la Vega for the purpose of the volume, the beginning invocation of the Virgin and the peroration (the *Nican tlantica*). Surveying the whole, one gets the impression that *nican tlaca* is used as a simple stylistic variant for *macehualtzitzintin*, which is somewhat but not inordinately more common in the texts. When the author wishes to be particularly resonant, he uses both expressions in tandem (pp. 56, 120, 124, accounting for three of the total of seven instances).

Our general feeling on the role of *nican tlaca* in the texts is that it has to do with the conservatism of ecclesiastical Nahuatl, which retained a certain amount of earlier usage far past the time when it was part of everyday Nahuatl speech. Since the sub-idiom was shared by Nahua secretary/consultants and Spanish priests, Laso de la Vega or an aide would have been equally likely to use the term.

Honorific terminology for the Virgin. When translating Nahuatl terms for Christian concepts and entities, one normally tries to reflect any marked difference from Christian notions that surfaces in a Nahuatl word. Thus we ordinarily put "God the child" rather than the expected "God the son" for *Dios tepiltzin*. These matters are, however, very tenuous and subtle. Some Nahuatl Christian terms seem to act as a prism through which Nahua ways of thought are expressed even within an originally European framework. Others look to be the result of a deliberate, clerically inspired effort to find an exact equivalent for a Spanish Christian word. Moreover, it is to be supposed that the inner meaning attached to the outer form approached ever closer to that of the Spanish original; surely Spaniards speaking Nahuatl would have used such words in that sense. Most of the Marian terminology seems of this type.

Cenquizcaichpochtli. The element *cenquizca* is the combining form of the preterit agentive noun *cenquizqui*, "something whole and perfect." It is often used quasi-independently with verbs in the sense "perfectly," but even more frequently it is incorporated, with an adjectival thrust, into a noun complex, as in Molina's *cenquizcamahuiçotl*, "perfect or consummate honor." *Ichpochtli* is "maiden," a female person who has reached puberty and is still unmarried. That it had the meaning "virgin" in preconquest times is hard to establish. Molina's gloss of Spanish *virgen* with "oc uel ychpochtli," "still really a maiden," or "still truly a maiden," implies that "virgin" was among the senses of the word but not the most current one. The term *cenquizcaichpochtli*, then, so frequently found in the Guadalupe texts, can be translated literally as "perfect (entire, untouched) maiden." In an earlier draft we translated it, with a bit of misgiving, as "immaculate Virgin," feeling that spotless is very close to perfect in this context. Being reminded by Louise Burkhart of our own principle of staying close to the original when it veers from the Spanish, we have settled on "consummate Virgin."

"Queen." The texts employ two Nahuatl constructions in this semantic range, differing only in which of two nominal elements, *cihuapilli*, "noblewoman," and *tlatoani*, "ruler," is subordinated to the other. Quite straightforward is *cihuapillatoani*, "noblewoman-ruler," which is virtually a Nahuatl gloss of what is meant by queen. The other term is *tlatocacihuapilli*, literally "ruler-noblewoman." In this formation one could take the *tlatoca-* element as adjectival, "rulerly noblewoman," and possibly arrive at a slightly different sense and translation. In our opinion, however, the closest equivalent is "queen" in both cases. That the intention of the two constructions is the same is hinted by their distribution, which does not follow noticeably varying semantic contexts but is determined by whether the word is possessed or not. When the term is possessed (nearly always in the first person plural, "our"), *cihuapillatoani* is used; when in the absolutive, *tlatocacihuapilli* appears.

Ilhuicac. By its elements this construction means literally "in the sky." "In heaven" is a very small stretch (after all, heaven and sky are the same in Spanish). In the Guadalupe texts it is used repeatedly as an attribute of the Virgin, and we have not hesitated to translate it "heavenly." We have not gone so far as to translate *ilhuicac tlatocacihuapilli* and related phrases as "Queen of heaven," although they are clearly filling that slot in church terminology and can be found so translated by Carochi.[1]

"Mother." The phrases describing the Virgin as mother present no strictly linguistic problems and are translated straightforwardly. *Totlaçonantzin*, "our precious Mother," is the approximate equivalent of Spanish *nuestra Señora* or English "our Lady," but we have not so translated it, since

---

[1]Carochi translates both "in ilhuicac cihuāpilli" (AC, f. 49v) and "in ilhuicac cihuāpillàtoāni" (f. 88v) as "la Reyna del cielo." The second phrase is also once translated simply as "Nuestra Señora." It would be easy to justify a translation of *ilhuicac tlatocacihuapilli* as "Queen of heaven." Whereas English readily produces such phrases as "king of France," Nahuatl has no such construction. When *tlatoani* is modified, it is most often preceded by a locative altepetl name, as in *Tetzcoco tlatoani*, which could be translated most directly as "ruler in Tetzcoco" or "Tetzcocan ruler," but with very little violence as "ruler of Tetzcoco." The positions and roles of *ilhuicac* and *tlatocacihuapilli* in the phrase which concerns us are closely analogous.

the difference and its implications are substantial, and the literal translation makes good English. Phrases describing the Virgin as the mother of God also appear, the two types alternating through the corpus. Overall, one must judge speaking of the Virgin as "our Mother" to have been an innovation of the Nahuas themselves; Spanish ecclesiastics, at least in earlier times, preferred other formulations. Laso de la Vega has given up any objection to the term, allowing it to be used in the general title of the work and many times throughout, including in his peroration (the *Nican tlantica)* and in the concluding prayer. It is a fact of interest, if hard to interpret, that the full form *totlaçonantzin* does not appear in the *Nican mopohua,* though the Virgin twice speaks of herself there as the mother of people, once in general and once of a specific person, Juan Diego (pp. 64, 78).

Mahuiz- , *mahuiztic.* The root *mahui-* has to do with fear, hence respect and wonderment. The derived *mahuiz-*, frequently used here in combining form with nouns referring to the Virgin, translates as "revered" and the like. The preterit agentive and in effect adjectival form *mahuiztic* means "splendid" or "wondrous." The related verb *mahuizoa* means in the first instance "to wonder at," but also occurs, often in tandem with the verb *itta,* as a more ornate synonym of "to see" and may be translated "to behold."

Tlaço- (tlaçò). This nominal root has the meanings "expensive, dear, fine," and the like. It was much used in combination with various nouns for relationships as an honorific in reference to Christian supernaturals, here the Virgin. We translate it "precious."

Other ecclesiastical terminology. By mid-sixteenth century or a little later, stable Nahuatl expressions had evolved for all the actions, concepts, objects, and personae involved in the daily practice of Spanish Christianity. They were used consistently in ecclesiastical circles, but had also penetrated the domain of everyday Nahuatl speech. How much of this vocabulary was actively invented by Spanish ecclesiastics, how much adapted by Nahua aides, and how much simply a part of the general evolution of contact phenomena among the Nahuatl speaking population as a whole is still the subject of investigation and need not concern us here. Some of the terms were loans, like *Dios,* "God," *cruz,* "cross," *misa,* "mass," or *sacristan,* "sacristan." Others were put together from Nahuatl elements, like *yolcuitia,* literally "to declare the heart," i.e., "to confess to a priest," *tetlamaca,* literally "to give something to someone, to serve someone food or drink," i.e., "to dispense communion," or *tlamahuiçolli,* literally "that which is marveled at," i.e., "miracle." All these and others like them are found in the Guadalupe texts, very much the same as they would be in any Nahuatl text of the time or for many decades previous. Some such terms, however, do have special nuances in the *Huei tlamahui-çoltica*.

Teocalli and teopan. Both of these words referred to temples in pre-conquest times and to Christian churches after the conquest. The primary original difference was perhaps that *teocalli* ("god-house") was applied more to the building and *teopan* (originating as a compound relational word, "god-at," "where the god is or gods are") more to the entire precinct. Even after the conquest, *teopan* was used both as a noun and as a locative expression. In general, *teopan* became much more common in postconquest times, but *teocalli* continued in use as an undercurrent and an alternative. To judge impressionistically from usage, it seems that *teopan* was mainly for larger churches, *teocalli* for smaller ones, chapels or dependencies.[1] Thus it is not unexpected that in the texts the predominant word for the chapel of Guadalupe is *teocalli*. Nevertheless, *teopan* also appears, and not only for a larger church like the one in Tlatelolco (p. 94), but also for the chapel of Guadalupe itself. The simple form of the word occurs only twice in this connection (pp. 54, 106), of which one instance seems to owe its existence to the need for a stylistic variant, but it occurs eight times, all in the *Nican motecpana*, in the modified form *iteopanchantzinco*, "in her churchly home."

Teopixqui. This word, literally "god-guardian," may or may not have been a postconquest neologism. In the course of the sixteenth century it came to be used overwhelmingly for friars, members of the mendicant orders, as opposed to secular priests, who were generally referred to by the Spanish loanword *clérigo*. In ecclesiastical circles, however, the scope of the term increasingly widened to include secular priests as well, and that is the usage found in the Guadalupe texts. We have thus translated "friar" or "priest" according to the interpretation dictated by the context.

Teoyotl. This abstract noun derived from *teotl*, "god," often had the specific meaning "sacrament(s) of the Christian church" in Nahuatl texts of the sixteenth and seventeenth centuries. Here, however, the meaning seems broader, closer to the original "divine or spiritual things, churchly matters," and we have translated it accordingly.

Caxtillan and related terms. Although the noun *Caxtillan* was the Nahuatl rendering of the Spanish Castilla, "Castile," in effect it meant "Spain." One of the first Spanish words to enter Nahuatl, it continued in use indefinitely. It is seen most often placed before another noun by way of modification, as in *Caxtillan xonacatl*, literally "Castile onion," i.e., garlic.

---

[1]See Lockhart 1992, pp. 536–37, n. 48.

In such constructions it can best be translated adjectivally, as "Spanish." The *Nican mopohua* contains several occurrences of *Caxtillan xochitl*, which by these principles should be "Spanish flower(s)." Molina, however, glosses the phrase as "rose," Sánchez speaks of roses in the parallel passages, and there is by now a long tradition of considering the miraculous flowers to have been roses. We cannot categorically assert that roses are not intended, but by emphasizing their diversity the text seems to aim at a broader meaning. Especially suggestive are two phrases on p. 84: "nepapã tlaçòxochitl in Caxtillancayotl," "various precious flowers in Spanish style," and "in ixquich nepapan Caxtillan xochitl," "all the different (types of) Spanish flowers." Thus we have translated "Spanish flower" and are by no means convinced that only roses are meant. One should also consider the propensity of older Spanish to use "roses" in a generic sense.

Caxtiltecatl derives from *Caxtillan* and means literally "inhabitant of Castile," hence "Spaniard." The term was widely used from an early time; it gradually made room for the loanword *español*, but never went entirely out of use. In the Guadalupe texts it is the predominant form, used several times in the *Nican motecpana*; *español*, however, does occur once in the *Nican tlantica*.

Yeppa. This word is known to Molina and Carochi as "previously, before," in effect often "always (in the past), already," and so it can be found in the Guadalupe texts as well (pp. 74, 76, 78, 82, 84, 116, 122). What we have not seen elsewhere (though it probably exists) is its use in connection with future-tense verbs in a meaning which we deduce from the context can only be something like "soon," "probably," "expectedly," even "before you know it." Instances of this type occur four times, twice in the *Nican mopohua* (pp. 74, 76) and twice in the *Nican motecpana* (pp. 54, 108). In all four cases the occurrence is something negative or feared, and three of the four involve the verb *miqui* "to die." Although we have found no support for this meaning in dictionaries and grammars, the context essentially allows no other interpretation, and we put it forward confidently.

Some final thoughts on the question of authorship

MODERN SCHOLARSHIP long tended unquestioningly to accept the Spanish ecclesiastics whose names are associated with Nahuatl texts of various kinds, from fray Pedro de Gante and Sahagún forward, as their authors. In the last fifteen years or so Nahuatl philologists have become ever more aware of the role of indigenous aides and have come to assume that a Nahua or team of Nahuas was most likely responsible for the composition of the final form of any polished text reaching us. The editors of the present volume share this assumption and believe that it is well grounded in general. The present case seems to represent an at least partial exception to the general tendency, especially if viewed in the context of the great age of production of Nahuatl texts in ecclesiastical circles, from the mid-sixteenth century until about the second decade of the seventeenth. Perhaps after that time fewer and less qualified indigenous aides were available and ecclesiastics were thrown more on their own in their Nahuatl undertakings.

At any rate, reviewing the situation at hand, we have seen here several different reasons to believe that Laso de la Vega was strongly, directly involved in the writing. What evidence do we have, beyond general expectations, of the participation of any native Nahuatl speakers at all, in any capacity? They were not needed to contribute any of the essential material, which is quite fully accounted for between Sánchez's work and various existing ecclesiastical texts containing the elements of Nahuatl polite conversation and sermonary conventions. They could not have been responsible for the morphological errors and Hispanic phrasing we have detected in many parts of the work. Indeed, one would not expect that an indigenous aide would have allowed any of the out-and-out errors to stand.

It is true that nothing at all is known about the procedures normally used by ecclesiastics and aides in cooperation on Nahuatl texts. We know only that errors like those in the Guadalupe texts are not otherwise seen. The general perfection of ecclesiastical Nahuatl writing in grammar and idiom leaves the impression that it was composed by Nahuas from the beginning, that they may have been reshaping material dictated to them or translating and adapting written Spanish texts before them, but that they were the only ones actually putting Nahuatl utterances on paper. It is entirely conceivable, however, that in some cases at least, the aide only emended utterances first committed to paper by the ecclesiastic. This is the only way in which indigenous participation could be reconciled with the nature of the Guadalupe texts as we know them. Even then, we would have to presume that the aide corrected only a certain number of errors, leaving others untouched. Perhaps he could have done so out of timidity or respect, or because of haste, or because he was not accustomed to reviewing manuscripts. The errors are after all mainly of a fairly subtle nature. But since other known comparable texts lack even such mistakes as these, we are left again wondering whether any indigenous correction took place at all.

Now the fact that sentences throughout the work betray the hand of some Spaniard, unamended by any native speaker, does not in itself prove that this Spaniard wrote the whole text. Utterances which pass muster as to idiom and grammar could still have been composed by a Nahua. They could equally well, of course, have been composed by a skillful Spaniard. Is there anything in the texts that one would tend to attribute specifically to a Nahua, something a Spaniard literate in Nahuatl would be unlikely to do? As it happens, ecclesiastical Nahuatl and ordinary elevated Nahuatl speech overlap extensively; "ecclesiastical Nahuatl" is indeed a version of elevated Nahuatl practiced, if not actually developed, by the aides as much as by the ecclesiastics. It is only when one sees usage more characteristic of mundane or less educated circles that one can at least strongly suspect the presence of a Nahua, not a Spaniard.

Little of this nature is to be found in the Guadalupe texts. On p. 104 the unorthodox "catcaya," a deviant, usually plebeian or provincial past tense of the verb *ca*, "to be," is distinctly not something one would expect from a Spanish priest. The variant *quepa* for *cuepa* (pp. 66, 68, and 72), "to turn," is rare even in mundane texts, but it can be found in modern spoken Nahuatl in some places.[1] A bit more ambiguous is the form "Españolestin," "Spaniards" (p. 118). It embodies a double plural specifically characteristic of Nahuatl speakers who were not yet fully apprised of the signs of the Spanish plural. Yet the double plural of this particular word became a very popular, long-lasting form to be seen in all sorts of Nahuatl texts, and there is no real reason Laso de la Vega might not have used it as he (along with Carochi and others) used *Caxtillan* even though he knew the Spanish form of the word. Another somewhat dubious case is "conittotihue" (p. 66), "that they go to tell him." This form occurs only once and differs from the standard only in the final letter, which is normally *i*, so that one might suspect that it is merely a typographical error. Yet the archaic *e* does appear in certain modern dialects of Nahuatl and was doubtless part of the speech of some provincial Nahuas in the seventeenth century.

Similar to these examples are the variant forms *miac* ("much") and *-ta* (past modal auxiliary), discussed above on p. 20. Found above all in the speech of provincial and less educated people, they too would be less likely to be used by a Spanish ecclesiastic. Here we have also the suggestive phenomenon of the use of both the standard and the variant form, *miec* as well as *miac*, *-tia* as well as *-ta*. The variation could easily be interpreted as the residue of the participation of two distinct hands, Laso de la Vega writing *miec* and *-tia*, the Nahua aide *miac* and *-ta*. It is also imaginable that the Nahua wrote the initial syllabic *y*'s in the text, Laso de Vega the *i*'s.

Virtually all of the nonstandard elements, phonetic and semantic, in the Guadalupe texts are attested in the Puebla/Tlaxcala/Huejotzingo region.

---

[1]Key and Key 1953, p. 193.

None of them are peculiar to that region, but in view of the overall impression one is left wondering if either Laso de la Vega had once served there or an aide of his came from that area.

If indeed there were two hands, they were intermingled. We have seen that the texts show a whole series of common characteristics from beginning to end; either the same individual or the same team produced them all. The strongest apparent evidence of collaboration, the varying forms just mentioned, appears in alternate succession literally on the same pages. The question is whether or not the variation could be the product of a single writer. Nahuatl texts do often show varying spelling conventions in the same document in a single hand and also insert or omit glides (*y* and *hu*) and glottal stop marking inconsistently. Phonetic variation such as that between *miec* and *miac*, with two different versions of a root-internal vowel, is rarer. That is not to say that it does not occur.[1]

The evidence, then, is not conclusive. The texts are surely compatible with the hypothesis of two writers, one doubtless Laso de la Vega and the other an indigenous aide. But there is nothing to preclude the possibility that Laso de la Vega, affected by the speech of areas where he had lived previously, was himself responsible for the variation. The very fact that he was, as the texts betray, not absolutely secure in matters of Nahuatl grammar and idiom is in itself a possible explanation of why things might vary.

Laso de la Vega's background in Nahuatl is a crucial factor which we have no way to judge except out of the texts themselves. To have produced the Guadalupe texts entirely alone, he would have had to have studied Nahuatl extensively (probably with the Jesuits, judging by his orthography) and to have an excellent knowledge of the existing body of ecclesiastical texts in the language. In a word, he would have had to be an expert philologist with accomplishments far beyond those of most of the priests of his time.[2] Yet no other sign of his erudition surfaces: no cross-references in other works, no accounts of his studying or teaching, no grammar, no sermonary, no confessional manual, nothing. In the present state of knowledge about the world of ecclesiastical Nahuatl philology in the sixteenth

---

[1]With precisely the root in question, a letter from Huejotzingo, dated 1560, all in the same hand, has an example of *miec* among several instances of *miac*, going from "miyacpa" to "miequi" and back to "miyaquinti" (Lockhart 1993, p. 292).

[2]And even beyond those of such a figure as Hernando Ruiz de Alarcón, who published a famous treatise on idolatry containing transcriptions and translations of numerous Nahuatl incantations (Ruiz de Alarcón 1984).

and seventeenth centuries, it is not at all impossible that such evidence should have disappeared. But one is left inclined to think after all that Laso de la Vega could hardly have performed the feat entirely by himself. Perhaps he first tried it alone, then sought help too late in the game for everything to be remedied. Perhaps the helper was himself much influenced by Spanish. These are matters for speculation, which with the resources presently available we cannot resolve. We are prepared to assert that by all indications Laso de la Vega took a large part in the composition of the Nahuatl texts in all sections of the work, but we cannot say with certainty whether he had collaborators or not.

Whoever was involved, some individual or team worked over the material thoroughly from beginning to end. After this process, one cannot speak with entire propriety of newer or older parts of the work. All parts are in some sense new, simply with different sources. For the apparition story and the miracle accounts, the most indicated source is the work of Sánchez, supplemented by the Stradanus engraving.[3]

---

[3]Some or all of the miracle stories may have been circulating orally in Spanish or Nahuatl through the early seventeenth century. But above we have shown the very high probability that Laso de la Vega and Sánchez used episodes in the exact order present in Stradanus. Whatever was used must have had an order identical to that of Stradanus and must have had very brief descriptions or captions. In other words, if it was not actually Stradanus it must have been an unknown proto-Stradanus or imitation of Stradanus no different from it in any essential way.

HVEI
TLAMAHVIÇOLTICA
OMONEXITI IN ILHVICAC TLATOCA-
ÇIHVAPILLI
SANTA MARIA
TOTLAÇONANTZIN
GVADALVPE IN NICAN HVEI ALTEPE-
NAHVAC MEXICO ITOCAYOCAN TEPEYACAC.

Impresso con licencia en MEXICO:
en la Imprenta de Iuan Ruyz.
Año de 1649.

BY A GREAT
MIRACLE APPEARED
THE HEAVENLY
QUEEN,
SAINT MARY,
OUR PRECIOUS MOTHER OF GUADALUPE,
HERE NEAR THE GREAT ALTEPETL OF MEXICO,
AT A PLACE CALLED TEPEYACAC.

*Printed with permission in MEXICO
in the press of Juan Ruiz,*
1649.

PARECER DEL P. BALTHASAR GONÇALEZ
de la Compañia de IESVS.
[*]

POR mandado del Señor Doctor Don Pedro de Barrientos Lomelin Comissario del Tribunal de la Santa Cruzada, Tesorero
desta Santa Cathedral de Mexico, Prouisor, y Vicario General de
su Arçobispado: he visto la milagrosa aparicion de la Imagen de
la Virgen Santissima Madre de Dios, y Señora Nuestra (q̃ se
venera en su Hermita,[1] y Santuario de Guadalupe.) que en
proprio, y elegante Idioma Mexicano, pretende dar à la Imprenta
el Bachiller Luys Lasso de la Vega, Capellan, y Vicario de dicho
Santuario. Hallo està ajustada à lo que por tradicion, y anales se
sabe del hecho, y por que serà muy vtil, y prouechosa para
aviuar la deuocion en los tibios, y engendrarla de nueuo en los
que ignorantes viuen del misterioso origen deste celestial retrato
de la Reyna del cielo, y porque no hallo cosa que se oponga à la
verdad, y misterios de nuestra Santa Fee, merece el encendido, y
affectuoso zelo, al mayor culto, y veneracion del Santuario que
es à su cargo del autor, se le dè la licencia que pide: assi lo
siento, y lo firmè de mi nombre en este Seminario de Naturales
del Señor San Gregorio, en 9. de Enero de 1649. Años.

Balthasar Gonçalez.

---

[1]The Spanish word *ermita*, by origin "hermitage," gained the additional
meaning of a small chapel, often in a rural setting, dedicated to a particular
saint whose image dominates it; the meaning is closely equivalent to what
today is called a chapel of ease.

- - - -
PACKING SLIP:
Amazon Marketplace Item: The Story of Guadalupe: Luis Laso
De LA Vega's Huei Tlamahuicoltica of 1649...
Listing ID: 0125L806203
SKU:
Quantity: 1

Purchased on: 24-Feb-2003
Shipped by: justkat82@aol.com
Shipping address:

Ship to: Albert Gomezplata
Address Line 1: 513 Powell Drive
Address Line 2:
City: Annapolis
State/Province/Region: Maryland
Zip/Postal Code: 21401
Country: United States

Buyer Name: secu visa

THE OPINION OF FATHER BALTASAR GONZÁLEZ
of the Society of JESUS.
[*]

BY ORDER of señor doctor don Pedro de Barrientos Lomelín, Commissary of the Tribunal of the Santa Cruzada, treasurer of this holy cathedral of Mexico, ecclesiastical judge and vicar general of its archdiocese, I have seen the miraculous apparition of the image of the Most Holy Virgin mother of God and our Lady (which is venerated in her *ermita*[1] and sanctuary of Guadalupe), which in correct and elegant Mexican language Bachelor Luis Laso de la Vega, chaplain and vicar of the said sanctuary, seeks to have printed. I find that it is in accord with what is known of the event by tradition and annals, and because it will be very useful and advantageous for enlivening the devotion of the lukewarm and regenerating it in those who live in ignorance of the mysterious origin of this celestial portrait of the Queen of heaven, and because I find nothing that is contrary to the truth and mysteries of our holy faith, the author's enthusiastic and heartfelt zeal for the greater worship and veneration of the sanctuary which is his responsibility makes him deserving to be given the permission that is asked. This is my opinion, and I signed it with my name in this seminary for natives of San Gregorio. January 9, 1649.

Baltasar González.

LICENCIA.

EN LA CIVDAD DE MEXICO A onze de Enero de mil y seiscientos y quarenta y nueue años. El Señor Doctor D. Pedro de Barrientos Lomelin, Tesorero en la Santa Iglesia Cathedral desta Ciudad, Prouisor, y Vicario General de este Arçobispado, &c. Auiendo visto el parecer del Padre Balthasar Gonçalez de la Compañia de IESVS, que es el de la foxa antes desta, y lo pedido por el Licenciado Luys Lasso de la Vega, Cura Vicario de la Hermita de Nuestra Señora de Guadalupe, extramuros desta dicha Ciudad: Dixo que daua, y diò licencia à qualquiera de los Impressores della, para que puedan imprimir el tratado de la Historia, y origen de la Santa Imagen de Nuestra Señora de Guadalupe, en lengua Mexicana, y assi lo proueyò, y firmò.

Doctor Don Pedro de Barrientos.

Ante mi Francisco de Bermeo, Notario Publico.

PERMISSION.

IN THE City of Mexico, January 11, 1649, señor doctor don Pedro de Barrientos Lomelín, treasurer in the holy cathedral church of this city, ecclesiastical judge and vicar general of this archdiocese, etc., having seen the opinion of Father Baltasar González of the Society of Jesus, which is the one on the preceding page, and the request by Licentiate Luis Laso de la Vega, vicar of the ermita of our Lady of Guadalupe outside the walls of this said city, said that he was giving and gave permission to any of the printers of the city to be able to print the treatise on the history and origin of the holy image of our Lady of Guadalupe in the Mexican language, and thus he decreed and signed it.

Doctor don Pedro de Barrientos.

Before me, Francisco de Bermeo, notary public.

ILHVICAC TLATÓCA-
ÇIHVAPILLE, ÇEMIHCAC ICHPOCHTZINTLÉ
in tiTlaçòmahuizNantzin in Dios.

[*]

MAÇIHVI càmo nolhuil àmo nomàcehual inic nonecuitlahuil mochiuh in moTeopantzin, in motlaçòCaltzin in oncan tictomahuiz-
tililìticate izçenquizca mahuiztililoni, in mixiptlatzin, ca ye otic-
mottilìtzino inic onimitznomaquili, onimitznohuenchihuilili in
noyollo niman in ìquac ononcalaquico in motlaçòchantzinco.
Auh inic çenca noconelehuia, noçenyollo ica nicnemilia, in mote-
quipanolocatzin, in momahuiztililocatzin, ca tepitzin ic nocon-
nextia in onocontlilan,[1] onoconìcuilo nahuatlàtolcopa in motlamahuiçoltzin: macamo quen xicmochihuili in mixtzin, in mo-
yecyollòtzin, ça yè xicmopaccaçelili in icnomaçehuallàtolli.[2] ca
oc hualca oticmochihuili in motetlaçòtlaliztzin inic itlatolcopa
oticmonochili, oticmonotzaltìtzino in icnomaçehualtzintli in itech
itilmàtzin, îayatzin xochahuiacatlapallotica, otimocopintzino, oti-
mìcuilòtzino, inic àmo mitzmotlànehuiliz; yequene inic qui-
caquiz, quimoyollotiz[3] in mìyotzin, in motlanequiliztzin. Auh
inic tiuhcatzintli nimitznottilia in càmo ticmotlàyelittilia in nepapan tlaca intlàtol, in ye tiquinmonotzaltìtzinoa, auh ca çenca ic
otiquinmoyollapanili inic omitzmiximachilìque, omitzmotepantla-
tòcatìtzinòque izçennohuian tlalticpac; Ca ye yèhuatl in onech-
yoleuh, in onechyolchicauh inic nahuatlàtolcopa onoconìcuilo in
çenca huei motlamahuiçoltzin inic otimoteittitìtzino, ihuan inic
oticmotemaquilìtia in mixiptlatzin in nicã motlaçòchantzinco
Tepeyacac ma oncã quittacan in maçehualtzitzintin, ma intlàtol-
tica quimatican in ixquich in impanpa oticmochihuili motetlaçòtlaliztzin, izçenca ic òpoliuhca[4] in cahuitl in iuhcatiliz, ihuan in
quen mochiuh.[5]

---

[1]*Onocontlilan*. This form is based on an unattested verb *tlilana*; Molina
gives only *tlilania*, "to trace or sketch" (VM, Nahuatl/Span., f. 147v),
which would make the present form *onocontlilani*. Other examples of *tlilana*
occur at notes 3, pp. 58–59, and 4, pp. 116–17.

[2]*Icnomaçehuallàtolli* is here translated literally as "humble commoner's
words." Molina defines *macehuallatoa* as "to speak in a rustic fashion" (VM,
Nahuatl/Span., f. 50v). Since it contains the additional root *icno-*, "poor,
humble," the term probably has to do primarily with polite self-effacement.
Yet something of the general ambiguity of *macehualli* (commoner, indigenous person) may apply here too. Laso de la Vega is emphasizing the use

O HEAVENLY QUEEN,
EVER VIRGIN, YOU WHO ARE THE
Precious Revered Mother of God.
[*]

ALTHOUGH I am unworthy that your church, your precious house, where we honor your perfect and wondrous image, has been given into my care, you have seen how at the very moment I came to enter your precious home I gave and offered my heart to you. Since I greatly desire, with all my heart, to ponder your service and the honor given you, I make known in a small way what I have traced[1] and written about your miracles in the Nahuatl language. Do not let your spirits be troubled, but gladly receive these humble commoner's words.[2] You have exercised your love in a greater way, when you summoned and called a poor humble commoner in his own language and made a copy of yourself and painted yourself with flowered fragrant hues on his mantle, his maguey cloak, so that he would not mistake you for any other and also so that he would hear and take to heart[3] your utterances and your wishes. And since that is the way you are, I see that you do not spurn the languages of different peoples when you summon them, and thereby you have greatly opened up their hearts so that they have recognized you and made you their intercessor everywhere on earth. That is what moved and encouraged me to write in the Nahuatl language the very great miracle by which you have appeared to people and have given them your image which is here in your precious home in Tepeyacac. May the humble commoners see here and find out in their language all the charitable acts you have performed on their behalf, [the memory of which] and their circumstances[5] had been lost according to the nature of time's passage.

---

of Nahuatl; *tlatolli* is the normal word for language, and in modern times at least, Nahuatl is sometimes called *macehualcopa* ("commoner-fashion"). Possibly the intention is "these poor words in an indigenous language."

[3]*Quimoyollotiz. Yollotia, nicno*, is glossed by Molina as to unburden oneself to someone, but in the present text it appears to have a more internal meaning, something like "take to heart." In this case it is used in tandem with *caqui*, "to hear or understand." Compare also at n. 7, pp. 100–01.

[4]*Ōpoliuhca*: The initial *o* is long, not followed by glottal stop. Possibly the intention was *ōpoliuhca*.

[5]*Ihuan in quen mochiuh*: literally, "and how it was done (or happened)."

Auh ca oc no centlamantli inic oniyoleuh inic oniyolchicauh nahuatlàtolcopa noconìcuiloz in motlamahuiçoltzin, auh ca yèhuatl
in quimìttalhuitzinoa in motlaçòtzin in motetequipanòcatzin S.
Buenaventura, ca in huei, in mahuiçauhqui, in huècapaniuhqui
itlamahuiçoltzin toTecuiyo Dios, nepapan tlàtoltica in mìcuiloz
inic quittazque, inic quimahuiçozq̃ in ixquichtin nepapan tlalticpac tlaca; In iuh mochiuh in ìquac[1] quauhnepanoltitech momiqui-
lìtzino in motlaçòconetzin, ca iquaicpactzinco ètlamātlàtoltica
huapaltitech omìcuilo in itzontequililocatzin, inic quittazq̃, qui-
mahuiçozq̃ nepapā tlàtoltica in nepapā tlaca izçenquizca huei,
izçẽquizca huècapaniuhqui, mahuiçoloni itetlaçòtlaliztzin inic
Cruztitech imiquizticatzinco oquinmomaquixtili izçemanahuac
tlaca. Auh ca no cenca huey, cenca huècapaniuhqui, cenca mahuiçoloni in mixiptlatzin in huel tèhuatzin momaticatzinco otic-
motlapalaquili, oticmìcuilhui in itechpatzinco ticmonequiltitzinoa
titotzàtzililizque[2] in timopilhuantzitzin, ilhuice in nican tlaca macehualtzitzintin in otiquinmottitìtzino. Ic ipampa ma nepapan tlàtoltica mìcuilo inic mochintin in nepapan tlàtoltica monotza quittazque, quimatizquè in momahuizçotzin, ihuan in çenca huey
motlamahuiçoltzin in inpampa oticmochihuili.

Auh intla nelli iuhqui, ca no tehuan tèhuatzin intloc, innahuac
timehuiltìticatca, in itlamachtiltzitzinhuan in motlaçòconetzin in
ìquac impantzinco ohualmehuitìtzino in Espiritu santo, in iuhquin tlexochnenepiltzintli ohualmocueptzinòtia[3] inic çeçeme
quinmotlaçòmacatzinoc[4] inic oquinmomachtili, inic oquinmaquili[5] in ixquich in nepapan tlàtolli inic çennohuian cemanahuac
omotemachtilito, oquimotecaquiztililito in ixquich in itlamahuiçoltzin in oquimochihuili in motlaçòconetzin auh ca tehuatzin oti-
quinmoyollalilìticatca, otiquinmoyolchicahuilìticatca in ìquac on;

---

[1]At this point the original has a marginal reference, partly cut off in the
copy we used, which seems to convey that the source was St. Bonaventure's
commentary on John 19.

[2]*Titotzàtzililizque.* This form lacks an object prefix; in the translation
we have presumed that the intention was *timitztotzàtzililizque,* "us to cry
out to you." However, elsewhere the text has the phrase *itech tzatzi,* "to cry
out to" (pp. 64, 94, 96, 98, 110, 112, 114). The error here might consist in
an extra *li,* in which case we would be dealing with intransitive *tzatzi* in the
reverential, not the applicative and transitive *tzatzilia.* One would also have
to make *itechpa* the equivalent of *itech,* the general connector of relational
words, although *itechpa* is usually more specific ("concerning," etc.); in
fact, the text has in one place the phrase *itechpatzinco motzatzilia* (p. 116).

There is also another thing from which I took heart and was encouraged to write your miracles in the Nahuatl language; it is what your beloved servant Saint Bonaventure says: that the great, marvelous, exalted miracles of our Lord God are to be written in a variety of languages so that all the different peoples on earth will see and marvel at them, as it happened when[1] your precious child died on the cross, and his sentence was written on a board above his head in three different languages so that different peoples in different languages would see and marvel at his altogether great and lofty, marvelous love by which he redeemed the peoples of the world through his death on the cross. Your image that you yourself colored and painted by your own hand is also very great, lofty, and wonderful; [through it you wish us your children to cry out to you],[2] especially the local people, the humble commoners to whom you revealed yourself. Therefore, let it be written in different languages so that all those who speak in different languages will see and know of your splendor and the very great miracle that you have worked on their behalf.

AND IF IT IS truly so, you were also seated close to and next to your beloved child's disciples when the Holy Spirit descended on them,[3] coming converted into something like tongues of fire in order to give each one of them his precious self and to teach them and give them all the different languages. With these they went all over the world to preach and to explain to people all the miracles that your precious child had worked. At that time you were consoling and encouraging them, and also by your peti-

---

The translation, instead of "through it you wish us your children to cry out to you," would then be "you wish us your children to cry out to it [the image]."

[3]At this point the original has the reference "Act. c. 1." in the margin.

[4]*Quinmotlaçòmacatzinoc, oquinmomacatzinoc.* In both of these forms the final *c* is erroneous. They should end in *o* (*ò*); although *c* is sometimes found in mundane texts indicating glottal stop, such is not a convention of the present text.

[5]*Oquinmaquili. Maca,* "to give something to someone," is a double-object verb, inherently applicative, and does not allow for an applicative suffix in the usual meaning. The applicative does frequently come in in combination with the reflexive prefix as the reverential. The intention here was thus doubtless *oquinmomaquili,* a reverential fully parallel with the verb immediately preceding.

auh in motlaìtlaniliztzin, in monemaçohualiztzin,[1] in motlatla-
tlauhtiliztzin ca ic oticmìcihuiltili, ca ic oticmonochilìtzino in
inpantzinco ohualmehuititzino in teotl Dios Espiritu santo, in
huel mopampatzinco oquinmomacatzinoc.[2]

Ma çanno iuhcatzintli inic nopan ximehuititzino ma nomàcehualti
in itlexochnenepiltzin inic nocontlilanaz[3] nahuatlàtolcopa in çenca
huei in motlamahuiçoltzin inic otiquinmottititzino icnomaçehual-
tzitzintin, yequene inic çenca huey tlamahuiçoltica otiquinmo-
maquilìtia i[4] mixiptlayotzin, auh intla motepalehuilizticatzinco itlà
ononhuelit ca maxcatzin, ca motlatquitzin, ma xicmopaccacelili.
Auh ca çan ixquich in, inic ye mocxitlantzinco nonnotlalchitlaça
in nimocnomaçehualtzin.

Bachiller Luys Lasso de la Vega.

---

[1]*Monemaçohualiztzin.* Reflexive *çohua* is attested in the meaning "to
exert oneself" (see ANS, p. 62). Nevertheless, with the addition of *ma-*,
"arm(s)", the reference is probably to spreading out the arms to implore,
especially in view of the surrounding nouns.

tioning, supplication,[1] and prayer you hastened and summoned the deity, God the Holy Spirit, to come upon them and give himself to them very much for your sake.

May he descend on me in the same way; may I receive his tongues of fire in order to trace[2] in the Nahuatl language the very great miracle by which you revealed yourself to the poor humble commoners and by which you also very miraculously gave them your image. If by your help I have been able to accomplish something, it belongs to you; kindly accept it. This is all with which I your humble subject now cast myself down at your feet.

Bachelor Luis Laso de la Vega.

---

[2]*Oquinmomacatzinoc*: see n. 4, p. 57.

[3]*Nocontlilanaz*: see p. 54, n. 1.

[4]*I*: for standard *in*, or possibly assimilated *im-*.

†

NICAN
MOPOHVA,
MOTECPANA IN QVENIN
YANCVICAN HVEI TLAMAHVIÇOLTICA
MONEXITI IN ÇENQVIZCAICHPOCHTLI
SANCTA MARIA DIOS YNANTZIN TOÇI-
HVAPILLATOCATZIN, IN ONCAN
TEPEYACAC MOTENEHVA
GVADALVPE.

Acattopa quimottititzino çe maçehualtzintli itoca
Iuan Diego; Auh çatepan monexiti in itlaçòIxiptlatzin
yn ixpan yancuican Obispo D. Fray Iuan de
Sumarraga. Ihuan in ixquich tlamahuiçolli ye
quimochihuilia.—

YE iuh màtlacxihuitl in opehualoc in atl in tepetl Mèxico,[1] yn ye
omoman in mitl, in chimalli, in ye nohuian ontlamatcamani in
ahuàcan, in tepehuàcan; in macaçan ye opeuh, ye xotla, ye
cueponi in tlaneltoquiliztli, in iximachocatzin in ipalnemohuani
nelli Teotl DIOS. In huel ìquac in ipan Xihuitl mill y quinientos,
y treinta y vno, quin iuh iquezquilhuioc in metztli Diziembre
mochiuh oncatca çe maçehualtzintli, icnotlàpaltzintli itoca catca
Iuan Diego, iuh mìtoa ompa chane catca in Quauhtitlan, auh in
ica Teoyotl oc moch ompa pohuia in Tlatilolco, auh Sabado catca
huel oc yohuatzinco, quihualtepotztocaya in Teoyotl, yhuan in
inetititlaniz; auh in àçico in inahuac tepetzintli in itocayòcan
Tepeyacac[2] ye tlatlalchipahua, concac in icpac tepetzintli cuicoa,
yuhquin nepapan tlaçototome cuica, cacahuani[3] in intozqui, iuhquin quinànanquîlia Tepetl, huel çenca teyolquimà, tehuel-

---

[1]*Mèxico*: for *Mexìco*.

[2]*Tepeyacac*: this proper name consists of *tepetl*, "mountain," *yacatl*,
"nose," and the relational word *-c*, "at." The term would generally be expected to mean a settlement on the ridge or brow of a hill. Since *yacatl* (the
nose going first) often implies antecedence, here the word may also refer to
the fact that the hill is the first and most prominent of a series of three.

[3]*Cacahuani.* This looks like a verb of the type that appears in three related forms: a basic one in *-ni*; an intransitive frequentative in *-ca*; and a

✝

HERE

IS RECOUNTED

AND TOLD IN AN ORDERLY FASHION
HOW BY A GREAT MIRACLE THE
CONSUMMATE VIRGIN SAINT MARY,
MOTHER OF GOD, OUR QUEEN,
FIRST APPEARED AT
TEPEYACAC, CALLED
GUADALUPE.

First she revealed herself to a humble commoner named Juan Diego, and afterwards her precious image appeared in the presence of the first bishop, don fray Juan de Zumárraga. And [here are related] all the miracles she has worked.

IT HAD been ten years since the altepetl of Mexico had been conquered and the weapons of war had been laid down, and peace reigned in the altepetls all around; likewise the faith, the recognition of the giver of life, the true deity, God, had begun to flower and bloom. Right in the year of 1531, just a few days into the month of December, there was a humble commoner, a poor ordinary person, whose name was Juan Diego. They say his home was in Cuauhtitlan, but in spiritual matters everything still belonged to Tlatelolco. It was Saturday, still very early in the morning, and he was on his way to attend to divine things and to his errands. When he came close to the hill at the place called Tepeyacac,[2] it was getting light. He heard singing on top of the hill, like the songs of various precious birds. Their voices were [swelling and fading?],[3] and it was as if the hill kept on

---

transitive frequentative in *-tza*. A verb *cahuani* (*cahuāni*) does indeed exist. DK (p. 21) shows it meaning "to catch fire" in a dialect of modern Nahuatl. Arthur J. O. Anderson (personal communication) knew it in the Sahagún corpus meaning "to flare, burst forth." These meanings are not what one expects from the context. If we search for a frequentative cognate of *cahuani*, we indeed find one: *cacahuaca*, which Molina defines as "gorgear a menudo las aves" (VM, Span./Nahuatl, f. 66); *Gorjear* is a general term which can mean any kind of bird sound. The related form *icahuaca* (*icahuaca*)

lâmachti in incuic, quiçenpanahuia in coyoltototl, in tzinitzcan,[1]
ihuan yn oc çequin tlaçòtotome ic cuica: quimotztimoquetz in
Iuan Diego quimòlhui[2] cuix nolhuil, cuix nomàçehual in ye nic-
caqui? àço çan nictemiqui? àço çan niccochtlehua, canin ye nicà,
canin ye ninotta, cuix ye oncan in in quìtotehuaque huehuetque
tachtohuan,[3] tocòcolhuan in xochitlalpan[4] in tonacatlalpan? cuix
ye oncan in in ilhuicatlalpan?

ompa onitztìcaya in icpac tepetzintli in tonatiuh iquîçayanpa in
ompa hualquiztia in ilhuicatlaçòcuicatl. auh in o yuh çeuhtiquiz
in cuicatl in omocactimoman in yèe[5] quicaqui hualnotzalo in
icpac tepetzintli, quilhuia Iuantzin Iuan Diegotzin; niman ça yeè[5]
motlapaloa inic ompa yaz in canin notzalo, àquen mochihua yn
iyollo, manoçe îtla ic miçahuia, yeçe huel paqui mohuellamach-
tia, quitlècahuìta[6] in tepetzintli, ompa itzta[6] in cãpa hualnotzaloc,

auh in ye àçitiuh in icpac tepetzintli, in ye oquimottili çe çihuapilli oncan moquetzinòticac,[7] quihualmonochili inic onyaz in
inahuactzinco; auh in o yuh àcito in ixpantzinco, cenca quimo-
mahuiçalhui in quenin huellaçenpanahuia inic çenquizcamahuiz-
ticatzintli, in itlaquentzin iuhquin tonatiuh ic motonameyotia inic

---

has the same definition without the frequentative sense (VM, ibid.). As an
impersonal (*tlacahuaca*), it refers to the murmuring or other noise of a
crowd, or the cries of massed enemies (VM, Nahuatl/Span., f. 115v).
Perhaps one is justified in drawing the conclusion that the family of words
refers primarily to massed or inchoate sound. It surely often appears in connection with birds. What we seem to have here is not a true frequentative,
but a normal reduplication, with glottal stop (the original does not specifically so indicate). The sense of this type of reduplication is broadly
distributive; here it would refer to the action stopping and starting again
various times. Thus though Velázquez's solution was morphologically
unsound (basing the form on transitive *cahua*), his notion that the meaning
was that the voices were alternately fading and intensifying (HT, p. 97, n.
32) may well be on the mark. We subscribe, provisionally, to the idea that
whatever the quality of sound meant, it was ebbing and flowing, which in
addition is consonant with the passage's sense of echo.
   [1]According to Sahagún (1981, 3:256), the bell bird (*coyoltototl* or pi-
ranga) is "like the thrushes mentioned previously, except that they have red
necks, breasts, and wings and the feathers are the same as the tail. Some of
them have yellow breasts and white wingtips and they sing very well. That
is why they are called coyoltotol, which means a bird that sings like a bell."
With regard to the *tzinitzcan*, he writes "there is a bird in this land that is

answering them. Their song was very agreeable and pleasing indeed, entirely surpassing how the bell bird, the trogon,[1] and the other precious birds sing. Juan Diego stopped to look, saying to himself, "Am I so fortunate or deserving as to hear this? Am I just dreaming it? Am I imagining it in sleepwalking? Where am I? Where do I find myself? Is it in the land of the flowers,[4] the land of plentiful crops, the place of which our ancient forefathers used to speak? Is this the land of heaven?"

He stood looking toward the top of the hill to the east, from where the heavenly, precious song was coming. When the song had subsided and silence fell, he heard himself being called from the top of the hill. A woman said to him, "Dear Juan, dear Juan Diego." Thereupon he stepped forward to go where he was summoned. His heart was not troubled, nor was he startled by anything; rather he was very happy and felt fine as he went climbing the hill, heading toward where he was summoned.

When he reached the top of the hill, he saw a lady standing there; she called to him to go over next to her. When he came before her, he greatly marveled at how she completely surpassed everything in her total splendor. Her clothes were like the sun in the way they gleamed and shone. Her resplendence struck the

---

called tzinitzcan or teutzinitzcan; this bird has black feathers and lives on the water; the precious feathers that it has grow on its breast and in its wingpits and under the wings; they are a mixture of resplendent black and green." Siméon gives a similar description, "a bird the size of a dove, whose very bright black plumage was used as an ornament and in different crafts" (DS, p. 662). Burkhart (1993, p. 3) identifies it with the Mexican trogon. See also Sahagún 1950–82, part 12 (Book 11).

[2]*Quimòlhui*: the *o* is neither long nor followed by a glottal stop.

[3]*Tachtohuan*: standard *tachtonhuan*, "our great-grandfathers."

[4]*Xochitlalpan*, a preconquest Nahuatl expression for heaven or a place of bliss. See Burkhart 1989, p. 76.

[5]*Yèe* and *yeè*. In both instances, an extra *e* has been added, apparently through simple error, to *ye*; in the first case the first of the two *e*'s bears a grave accent, in the second case the second one. Both times the intention seems to be *ye*, "already," rather than *yè*, third person independent pronoun.

[6]*-Ta* is a variant of preterit progressive *-tia (-tiyà)*. Both forms occur in the present text.

[7]*Moquetzinòticac*. This could have been written *moquetztzinòticac*, representing all the elements of the constituent roots, but in fact it was more common, even in the strictest orthographies, to write only one *tz* where two met, reflecting Nahuatl speech patterns.

pepetlaca; auh in tetl, in texcalli inic itech moquetza, inic quimina
in itlanexyotzin yuhqui in tlaçòchalchihuitl, maquiztli; inic neci
yuhquin ayauhcoçamalocuecueyoca in tlalli; auh in mizquitl, yn
nòpalli, ihuan oc cequi nepapan xiuhtotontin oncan mochìchi-
huani yuhquin quetzalitztli, yuhqui in teoxihuitl in iatlapallo ic
neci; auh in iquauhyo, in ihuitzyo, in iàhuayo yuhqui in coztic
teocuitlatl ic pepetlaca.

Ixpãtzinco mopechtecac, quicac in iyotzin, in itlàtoltzin in huel
çenca tehuellamachti, in huel tecpiltic yuhqui in quimoçòçonahuilia,[1] quimotlatlaçotilia, quimolhuili, tla xiccaqui noxocoyouh Iuantzin campa in timohuica? auh in yèhuatl quimonanquilili Notecuiyoe, Çihuapillè Nochpochtzinè[2] ca ompa nonàçiz
mochantzinco[3] Mexico Tlatilolco, nocontepotztoca in teoyotl, in
techmomaquilia, in techmomachtilia in ixiptlahuan in tlacatl in
Totecuiyo, in toteopixcahuan.

Niman ye ic quimononochilia, quimixpatilia[4] in itlaçòtlanequi-
liztzin, quimolhuilia,

Ma xicmati, ma huel yuh ye in moyollo noxocoyouh ca nèhuatl in niçẽquizcaçemìcacichpochtli Sancta Maria in ninantzin in huel nelli Teotl Dios in ipalnemohuani, in teyocoyani,
in Tloque Nahuaque, in Ilhuicahua in Tlalticpaque, huel nic-
nequi, cenca nîquelehuia inic nican nechquechilizque noteo-
caltzin in oncan nicnextiz, nicpantlaçaz, nictemacaz in ixquich notetlaçotlaliz, noteicnoyttaliz, in notepalehuiliz, in no-
temanahuiliz canel nèhuatl in namoicnohuàcanantzin in tèhuatl ihuan in ixquichtin inic nican tlalpan ançepantlaca,
ihuan in oc çequin nepapan tlaca notetlaçotlacahuan in notech
motzatzilia, in nechtèmoa[5] in notech motemachilia,[6] ca on-

---

[1]*Quimoçòçonahuilia.* According to Molina (VM, Nahuatl/Span., f. 23v),
this verb is *coconahuilia.*

[2]*Nochpochtzinè.* Meaning literally "my daughter," as we have been
forced to translate it, this is nevertheless, in the context, an expression of
great respect.

[3]*Mochantzinco*: to refer to a distant place as the home of the interlocutor
was another device of polite speech in older Nahuatl.

[4]*Quimixpatilia*: for *quimixpantilia* (probably a case of a missing tilde
over the first *a*).

[5]*Nechtèmoa*: the *e* is neither long nor followed by glottal stop.

[6]*Motemachilia. Temachia* is a common transitive verb meaning, generally, "to trust, have confidence in," and sometimes "to have need of" (VM,
Nahuatl/Span., f. 96; Span./Nahuatl, f. 88v). The "trust" sense is entirely

stones and boulders by which she stood so that they seemed like precious emeralds and jeweled bracelets. The ground sparkled like a rainbow, and the mesquite, the prickly pear cactus, and other various kinds of weeds that grow there seemed like green obsidian, and their foliage like fine turquoise. Their stalks, their thorns and spines gleamed like gold.

He prostrated himself before her and heard her very pleasing and courtly message, as if inviting and flattering him, saying to him, "Do listen, my youngest child, dear Juan, where is it that you are you going?" He answered her, "My patron, noble lady, my daughter,[2] I am going to your home[3] of Mexico-Tlatelolco. I am pursuing the divine matters that the representatives of the lord our Lord, our friars, give and teach us."

Thereupon she conversed with him, revealing to him her precious wish. She said to him,

Know, rest assured, my youngest child, that I am the eternally consummate virgin Saint Mary, mother of the very true deity, God, the giver of life, the creator of people, the ever present, the lord of heaven and earth. I greatly wish and desire that they build my temple for me here, where I will manifest, make known, and give to people all my love, compassion, aid, and protection. For I am the compassionate mother of you and of all you people here in this land, and of the other various peoples who love me, who cry out to me, who seek me, who trust in me.[6] There I will listen to their weeping and their sorrows in order to remedy and heal all

---

appropriate in the present context, giving us excellent reason to think that *temachia* is indeed intended, but here, since the reflexive *mo-* and the applicative *-lia* cancel each other out as the reverential, it is construed as intransitive, or as a verb *machia* with the indefinite personal object *te-*, which comes to the same thing. Such characteristics of the verb are nowhere attested, and though this is no simple error, for the writer of the present text apparently repeats the construction elsewhere (at n. 1, pp. 118–19), it is quite implausible. *Temachia* shows every sign of being derived from the transitive verb *mati*, "to know". *-Machia* (apparently a shortened version of the applicative *machilia*) therefore automatically requires two objects, one being the incorporated *te-*, leaving another to be accounted for by some specific object prefix.

can niquincaquiliz in inchoquiz, in intlaocol inic nicyectiliz, nicpàtiz in ixquich nepapan innetoliniliz, intonehuiz, inchichinaquiliz. Auh inic huel neltiz in nicnemìlia[1] inin noteicnoyttaliz ma xiauh in ompa in itecpãchan in Mexìco Obispo, auh tiquilhuiz in quenin nèhua nimitztitlani inic ticyxpantiz in quenin huel çenca nicelehuia inic ma nican nechcalti, nechquechili in ipan in tlalmantli noteocal; huel moch ticpohuiliz in ixquich in otiquittac, oticmahuiçò, ihuan in tlein oticcac; auh ma yuh ye in moyollo ca huel nictlaçòcamatiz, auh ca niquixtlahuaz, ca ic nimitzcuiltonoz, nimitztlamachtiz, yhuã miec oncan ticmàçehuaz ic nicquepcayotiz[2] yn mociahuiliz in motlatequipanoliz inic ticnemilitiuh[1] in tlein ic nimitztitlani: ò[3] ca ye oticcac noxocoyouh yn nìiyo in notlàtol ma ximohuicatiuh[4] ma ixquich motlàpal xicmochihuili.
Auh niman ic ixpantzinco onmopechtecac quimolhuili notecuiyoè, Çihuapillè ca ye niyauh in nicneltiliz, in miyòtzin, in motlàtoltzîn, ma oc nimitznotlalcahuili in nimocnomaçehual. Niman ic hualtemoc inic quineltilitiuh in inetitlaniz connamiquîco in cuepòtli huallamelahua Mexico.

In oàcico ìtic altepetl, niman ic tlamelauh in iTecpanchantzinco Obispo in huel yancuican hualmohuicac Teopixcatlàtohuani[5] itocatzin catca, D. Fray Iuan de Sumarraga S. Francisco Teopixqui. Auh in oàcito niman ic moyèyecoa inic quimottiliz, quîntlatlauhtia in itetlayecolticahuan, in itlannencahuan inic conittotihue,[6] ye achi huècauhtica in connotzaco, in ye omotlanahuatili in Tlàtohuani Obispo inic calaquiz. Auh in oncalac niman ixpantzinco motlanquaquetz, mopechtecac, niman ye ic quimixpantilia quimopohuililia yn ìyotzin yn itlàtoltzin ilhuicac

---

[1]The verb *nemilia* has very different glosses in different forms: to consider, to look into, to maintain, to resolve (VM, Nahuatl/Span., f. 67; DK, p. 165). Glosses in available dictionaries do not seem to exhaust the word's meaning. We take it that it goes back to *nemi*'s ancient sense of motion and can refer either to revolving something in the mind or to putting something into motion in a variety of contexts. The first of the present two examples (*in nicnemìlia*), which we have translated "which I am contemplating," may mean "which I am implementing." The second example (*ticnemilitiuh*), here translated "you go to put into motion," clearly refers to the plane of action. In *nicnemìlia*, the *i* bearing a grave accent is neither long nor followed by a glottal stop.

their various afflictions, miseries, and torments. And in order that this my act of compassion which I am contemplating[1] may come to pass, go to the bishop's palace in Mexico and tell him how I am sending you to put before him how I very much wish that he build me a house, that he erect a temple for me on the level ground here. You are to relate every single thing that you have seen and beheld, and what you have heard. And rest assured that I will be very grateful for it, and I will reward it, for I will enrich you and make you content for it. You will attain many things as my repayment for your efforts and labors with which you go to put in motion[1] what I send you for. And so, my youngest child, you have heard my message. Get on your way, make every effort.

Thereupon he prostrated himself before her, saying to her, "My patron, O Lady, now I am going to carry out your message. Let me, your humble subject, take leave of you for a while." Thereupon he came back down in order to go carry out his errand, coming to take the causeway that comes directly to Mexico.

WHEN HE got inside the altepetl, he went straight to the palace of the bishop, whose name was don fray Juan de Zumárraga, a friar of Saint Francis and the very first priestly ruler[5] to come. As soon as he arrived, he attempted to see him; he implored his servants and dependents to go tell him. After a rather long time they came to tell him that the lord bishop had given orders for him to enter. When he came in, he knelt and bowed low before him. Then he put before him and told him the heavenly Lady's message, his errand. He also told him everything that he had

---

[2]*Nicquepcayotiz*: standard *niccuepcayotiz*. The text has *q* for *c* in the root *cuepa* "to return" two other times, in addition to many instances of the standard spelling.

[3]*Ò ca*: the *o* is long and is not followed by glottal stop.

[4]*Ximohuicatiuh*: Following Carochi (AC, f. 28v), this form, which involves the singular optative of a purposive-motion suffix, should be *ximohuicà* or *ximohuicati*. See also pp. 86–87, n. 4.

[5]*Teopixcatlàtohuani*, "priestly ruler"; i.e., bishop.

[6]*Conittotihue*: the plural of the modal form of *yauh* standardly ends in *i* (*i*), but *e* is found in some varieties of modern Nahuatl and presumably has existed for centuries.

Çihuapilli, in inetitlaniz: no ihuan quimolhuilia in ixquich oquimahuiçò, in oquittac, in oquicac. Auh in oquicac in mochi itlatol,
inetitlaniz iuhquin àmo çenca monelchiuhtzino, quimonanquilili,
quimolhuili nopiltzè ma oc çeppa tihuallaz, oc ihuian nimitzcaquiz, huel oc itzinècan niquittaz, nicnemiliz in tlein ic otihualla
in motlanequiliz, in motlaelehuiliz. Hualquiz tlaocoxtihuitz, inic
àmo nimam[1] oneltic in inetitlaniz.

Niman hualmoquep[2] izça ye ìquac ipan çemilhuitl, niman
oncã huallamelauh in icpac tepetzintli, auh ipantzinco àçito in
ilhuicac Çihuapilli izçan ye oncan in canin acattopa quimottili,
quimochialitica; auh in o iuh quimottili ixpantzinco mopechtecac
motlalchitlaz quimolhuili,

notecuiyoè, tlacatlè, Çihuapillè, noxocoyohuè, Nochpochtzinè ca onihuia in ompa otinechmotitlanili, ca onicneltilito in
mìyotzin in motlàtoltzin maçihui in ohuìhuitica[3] in onicalac
in ompa iyeyan teopixcaTlàtohuani, ca oniquittac, ca ò[4] ixpan nictlali in mìyotzin, in motlàtoltzin in yuh otinechmonànahuatili, onechpaccacelì, auh ôquiyeccac; yece inic onechnanquili, yuhquin àmo iyollo ômàcic, àmo monelchihua,[5]
onechilhui oc ceppa tihuallaz, oc ihuiyan nimitzcaquiz, huel
oc itzinècan niquittaz in tlein ic otihualla motlayelehuiliz,[6]
motlanequiliz. Huel itech oniquittac in yuh onechnanquili ca
momati in moteocaltzin ticmonequiltia mitzmochihuililizñ
nican àço çan nèhuatl nicyòyocoya, acaçomo motencopatzinco; ca çenca nimitznotlatlauhtilia notecuiyoè, Çihuapillè
Nochpochtzinè manoço àca[7] çeme in tlaçòpipiltin in iximacho, in ixtilò, in mahuiztilò itech xicmocahuili in quitquiz,
yn quihuicaz in mìyotzin, yn motlàtoltzin, inic neltocoz,
canel[8] nicnotlapaltzintli, ca nimecapalli, ca nicacaxtli, ca nicuitlapîlli, ca natlapalli, ca nitconi cà[9] nimamaloni, càmo no-

---

[1]*Nimam*: standard *niman*.
[2]*Hualmoquep*: standard *hualmocuep*; see pp. 66–67, n. 2.
[3]*Ohuìhuitica*: This seems to be based on a confusion of *ohuì*, "difficult,
dangerous," and *ihuihuì* (*ihuīhui*), "with much difficulty, at great cost" (AC,
f. 121v). It is more than one individual's error, however, for Carochi in-
forms us that once in a while someone would say *ohuìhuìcayotica* instead of
ihuihuìcayotica, although he did not approve of it. The more standard form
ohuìtica appears below.
[4]*Ò*: the *o* is long and not followed by a glottal stop.
[5]Neither *-yollo maci* nor *nelchihua, nino*, have known dictionary glosses
corresponding to their use in the present text, in which they appear as

beheld, what he had seen and heard. But when he had heard his whole statement and message, he did not seem to be completely convinced. He answered him, telling him, "My child, do come again, and I will hear you at length. First I will thoroughly look into and consider what you have come about, your wish and desire." He came back out grieving, because his errand was not then carried out.

HE CAME BACK right away, on the very same day. He came straight to the top of the hill and found the heavenly Lady in the same place where he first saw her, waiting for him. When he saw her, he bowed low before her and threw himself to the ground, saying to her:

My patron, O personage, Lady, my youngest child, my daughter, I went to where you sent me, I went to carry out your instructions. Although it was difficult[3] for me to enter the quarters of the priestly ruler, I did see him, and I put before him your message as you ordered me to. He received me kindly and heard it out, but when he answered me, he did not seem to be satisfied or convinced.[5] He told me, "You are to come again, and I will hear you at leisure. First I will thoroughly look into what you have come about, your wish and desire." I could easily see from how he answered me that he thought that perhaps I was just making it up that you want them to build your temple there for you and that perhaps it is not by your order. I greatly implore you, my patron, noble Lady, my daughter, entrust one of the high nobles, who are recognized, respected, and honored, to carry and take your message, so that he will be believed. For[8] I am a poor ordinary man, I carry burdens with the tumpline and carrying frame, I am one of the common people, one

---

synonyms (here in tandem) where the context strongly demands the meaning to be satisfied with or convinced of the truth of something. The literal meaning of the roots lends support to the implications of the context: *-yollo maci*, "for one's heart to reach itself, be complete"; reflexive *nelchihua*, "to make oneself true."

[6]*Motlayelehuiliz*: standard *motlaelehuiliz*, as it is in the text several lines above (though inserted intervocalic glides are rife in Nahuatl speech and in older Nahuatl writing).

[7]*Àca*: for *acà*.

[8]The following phrases are standard Nahuatl metaphors for commoners.

[9]*Cà*: the *a* is short and not followed by a glottal stop.

nènemian, càmo nonequetzayan in ompa tinechmihualia
Nochpochtzinè, Noxocoyohuè, Tlacatlè, Çihuapillè, ma xi-
nechmotlapopolhuili nictequipachoz in mixtzin, in moyollotzin, ipan niyaz, ipan nihuetziz in moçomaltzin, in moqualantzin Tlacatlè Notecuiyoè.

Quimonanquilili izçenquizcamahuizichpochtzintli
tla xiccaqui noxocoyouh ma huel iuh ye in moyollo càmo
tlaçotin in notetlayecolticahuan in notìtitlanhuan, in huel
intech niccahuaz in quitquizq̃ in nìiyo, in notlàtol, in
quineltilizque in notlanequiliz; yece huel iuh monequi inic
huel tèhuatl ic tinemiz, ipan titlàtoz, huel momatica neltiz
mochihuaz, in noçializ, in notlanequiliz; auh huel nimitz-
tlatlauhtia noxocoyouh, yhuan nimitztlaquauhnahuatia ca
huel oc çeppa tiaz in moztla tiquittatiuh in Obispo auh
nopampa xicnèmachti, huel yuh xiccaquiti in noçializ, in
notlanequiliz, inic quineltiliz in quichihuaz noteòcal niquìtlanilia, yhuan huel oc ceppa xiquilhui in quenin huel nèhuatl
niçemìcacichpochtli Sancta Maria in ninantzin Teotl Dios in
ompa nimitztitlani.

Auh in Iuan Diego quimonanquilili, quimolhuili
notecuiyoè, Çihuapillè, Nochpochtzinè macamo nictequipacho in mixtzin, in moyollotzin ca huel noçenyollocacopa
nonyaz noconnelteltitiuh in mìiyotzin in motlàtoltzin ca niman
àmo nicnocacahualtia, manoçe nictecococamati in òtli ca
nonyaz ca noconchihuatiuh in motlanequiliztzin, çan huel ye
in àçocàmo[1] niyeccacòz;[2] intla noce ye onicacoc àcaçomo
nineltocoz, ca tel moztla ye teotlac in ye oncalaqui tonatiuh,
niccuepaquiuh in mìiyotzin in motlàtoltzin in tlein ic nechnanquiliz in Teopixcatlatohuani, ca ye nimitznotlalcahuilia
noxocoyohuè, Nochpochtzinè tlacatlè, Çihuapillè, ma oc
ximoçehuìtzino,

Niman ic ya in ichan moçehuito.
    Auh in imoztlayoc Domingo huel oc yohuatzinco tlàtlayohua-
toc ompa hualquiz in ichan huallamelauh in Tlatilolco, quimat-
tihuitz in Teoyotl, ihuan inic tèpohualoz:[3] niman yè inic quittaz
Teopixcatlàtohuani; auh àço ye ipan màtlactli hora in ôneçen-
cahualoc inic omocac Missa, ihuan otepohualoc ic hualxin in

---

[1]*Àçocàmo*: apparently an error for *àcaçomo* as just below.
[2]*Niyeccacòz*: the *o* is long but is not followed by glottal stop.
[3]*Tèpohualoz*: the *e* is long but is not followed by glottal stop. The

who is governed. Where you are sending me is not my usual place, my daughter, my youngest child, O personage, O Lady. Pardon me if I cause you concern, if I incur or bring upon myself your frown or your wrath, O personage, O my Lady.

The revered consummate Virgin answered him,

Do listen, my youngest child. Be assured that my servants and messengers to whom I entrust it to carry my message and realize my wishes are not high ranking people. Rather it is highly necessary that you yourself be involved and take care of it. It is very much by your hand that my will and wish are to be carried out and accomplished. I strongly implore you, my youngest child, and I give you strict orders that tomorrow you be sure to go see the bishop once again. Instruct him on my behalf, make him fully understand my will and wish, so that he will carry out the building of my temple that I am asking him for. And be sure to tell him again how it is really myself, the ever Virgin Saint Mary, the mother of God the deity, who is sending you there.

Juan Diego answered her, saying to her,

My patron, O Lady, my daughter, let me not cause you concern, for with all my heart I will go there and carry out your message. I will not abandon it under any circumstances; although I find the road painful, I will go to do your will. The only thing is that I may not be heard out, or when I have been heard I may not be believed. However, tomorrow, late in the afternoon, when the sun is going down, I will come returning whatever answer the priestly ruler should give me to your message. Now, my youngest child, my daughter, O personage, O Lady, I am taking leave of you; meanwhile, take your rest.

Thereupon he went home to rest.

ON THE FOLLOWING day, Sunday, while it was still very early in the morning and dark everywhere, he left his home and came directly to Tlatelolco to learn divine things and to be counted,[3] and also to see the priestly ruler. It was perhaps ten o'clock when they were finished with hearing mass and taking the

_____

literal meaning is "for people to be counted"; in the early period the friars are said to have kept detailed records of attendance at mass and instructions.

ichquich[1] maçehualli; auh in yèhuatl Iuan Diego niman ic yà in
itecpanchantzinco in Tlàtohuani Obispo, auh in ôàcito ixquich
itlàpal quichiuh inic quimottiliz, auh huel ohuìtica in oc çeppa
quimottili, icxitlantzinco motlanquaquetz, choca, tlaocoya inic
quimononochilia, inic quimixpantililia in iïyotzin, in itlàtoltzin in
ilhuicac Çihuapilli, inic àço çanen[2] neltocoz in inetitlaniz in itlanequiliztzin çenquizcaichpochtli, inic quimochihuililizque, inic
quimoquechililizque in iteòcaltzin in canin omotlatenehuili in
canin quimonequiltia. Auh in Tlatohuani Obispo huel miactlamantli[3] inic quitlàtlani, quitlatemoli, inic huel iyollo màciz, campa in quimottili, quenamècatzintli huel moch quimopohuilili in
Tlàtohuani Obispo. Auh maçihui in huel moch quimomelahuilili
in yuhcatzintli, ihuan in ixquich oquittac, oquimahuiçò in ca huel
yuh neci ca yèhuatzin izçenquizcaIchpochtzintli in itlaçòmahuiznanzin[4] in toTemaquixticatzin toTecuiyo Iesu Christo; yece àmo
niman ic omonelchiuh quìtto ca àmo çan ica itlàtol, itlaìtlaniliz
mochihuaz moneltiliz in tlein quìtlani, ca huel oc itlà inezca
monequi inic huel neltocoz in quenin huel yèhuatzin quimo-
titlanilia in ilhuicac Çihuapilli. Auh in ô yuh quicac in Iuan Diego
quimolhuili in Obispo tlacatlè, tlatohuaniè ma xicmottili catlèhuatl yez in inezca ticmìtlanililia, ca niman niyaz nicnìtlanililitiuh
in ilhuicac cihuapilli onechhualmotitlanili. Auh in ôquittac in
Obispo ca huel monelchihua ca niman àtle ic meleltia,[5]
motzotzona niman ic quihua.

Auh in ye huitz niman ic quimonahuatili quezqui in ichan tlaca,
in huel intech motlacanequi, quihualtepotztocazque, huel quipì-
piazque campa in yauh, ihuan aquin conitta, connotzà.[6] Tel iuh
mochiuh[7] auh in Iuan Diego niman ic huallamelauh, quitocac in
cuepòtli, auh in quihualtepotztocaya oncan atlauhtli quiça i-
nahuac tepeyacac quauhpantitlan quipoloco, manel oc nohuian
tlatemòque aoccan quittaque, çan yuh hualmoquepquè,[8] àmo

---

[1]*Ichquich*: for *ixquich*.

[2]*Çanen*: presumably the same as *çannen*, "in vain" (VM, Nahuatl/
Span., f. 14v); here it seems to amount to a simple negative.

[3]*Miactlamantli*: *miac* is an older variant of *miec*, "much," seen several
times in the text.

[4]*Itlaçòmahuiznanzin*: for *itlaçòmahuiznantzin*.

[5]*Meleltia*: standard *mellltia*. Among the meanings of *elleltia*, *nino*, is

count, and all the commoners dispersed again. Thereupon Juan
Diego went to the palace of the lord bishop; when he got there,
he made every effort to see him, but it was with great difficulty
that he saw him again. He knelt down at his feet, and he wept
and grieved as he told and put before him the message of the
heavenly Lady, because he wondered if perhaps the consummate
Virgin's message and will that they were to build and erect a
temple for her where she designated and wanted it would not[2] be
believed. The lord bishop asked and interrogated him about very
many things in order to be satisfied about where he saw her and
what she was like, and he told it absolutely all to the lord
bishop. Although he told him the exact truth about how she was
and all that he had seen and beheld, and that she really seemed to
be the consummate Virgin, the precious, revered mother of our
redeemer, our lord Jesus Christ, still he was not immediately
convinced. He said that it was not by his [Juan Diego's] word
and request alone that what he asked for would be done and
carried out. Some additional sign was still very much needed so
that it could be believed that it was really the heavenly Lady
herself who sent him. When Juan Diego heard that, he said to
the bishop, "O personage, O ruler, consider what kind of sign it
is to be that you request of her, and then I will go ask it of the
heavenly Lady who sent me here." And when the bishop saw
that he was entirely convinced, that he had absolutely no second
thoughts[5] or doubts, he thereupon sent him off.

And when he was on his way, thereupon he [the bishop]
ordered some of the people of his household in whom he had
full confidence to follow after him and keep close watch where
he went, whom he saw, and whom he talked to. But it so happened[7] that thereupon Juan Diego came straight along the causeway, and those who came following him lost sight of him at the
place where the ravine comes out near Tepeyacac, next to the

"to repent of something" (VM, Nahuatl/Span., f. 28v).

[6]*Connotzà*: the *a* is short and not followed by a glottal stop.

[7]*Tel iuh mochiuh*. The translation "but it so happened [that]" is quite
straightforward. Yet *tel*, like French *mais*, does not always imply a sharp
contrast with what precedes. An alternate translation might be "And so it
was done; but . . ."

[8]*Hualmoquepquè*: standard *hualmocuepquè*; see pp. 66–67, n. 2.

çaniyo inic omoxixiuhtlatito, no ihuan ic oquimelelti,¹ oquin-
qualancacuiti:² yuh quinonotzato in Tlàtohuani Obispo, quitla-
huellalilique³ inic àmo quineltocaz, quilhuiq̃ inic çan conmoz-
tlacahuilia, çan quipìpiqui in tlein quihualmolhuilia, ànoçe çan
oquîtemic, çan oquîcochìtleuh in tlein quimolhuilia in tlein qui-
mìtlanililia; auh huel yuh quîmolhuique intla oc ceppa huallaz,
mocuepaz, oncan quitzitzquizque, ihuan chicahuac quitlatzacuil-
tizque inic aocmo çeppa iztlacatiz, tèquamanaz.⁴

    In imoztlayoc Lunes in ìquac quihuicazquia in Iuan Diego in
ìtla⁵ inezca inic neltocoz, aocmo ohualmocuep: yeica in ìquac
àçito in ichan çe ìtla⁶ catca itoca Iuan Bernardino o itech motlali
in cocoliztli, huel tlanauhtoc, oc quiticinochilito, oc ipan tlàto,⁷
yece aocmo inman ye huel otlanauh: auh in ye yohuac quitla-
tlauhti in iTla in oc yohuatzinco, oc tlàtlayohuatoc hualquiçaz,
quimonochiliquiuh in oncan Tlatilolco çeme in teopixque inic
mohuicaz, quimoyolcuitilitiuh, ihuan quimoçencahuilitiuh, yeica
ca huel yuh ca in iyollo ca ye inman, ca ye oncan inic miquiz ca
aoc mehuaz aocmo pàtiz.

    Auh in Martes huel oc tlàtlayohuatoc in ompa hualquiz ichan
in Iuan Diego in quimonochiliz teopixqui in ompa Tlatilolco, auh
in ye àçitihuitz inahuac tepetzintli tepeyacac in icxitlan quiztica
òtli tonatiuh icalaquianpa in oncan yeppa quiçani, quìto intla çan
nicmelahua òtli manen nechhualmottilìti izçihuapilli ca yeppa

---

¹*Omoxixiuhtlatito, . . . oquimelelti*: the second word would standardly
be written *oquimellelti. Xiuhtlatia, nino*, is once defined by Molina as "to
get vexed over delay" (VM, Span./Nahuatl, f. 53v); a meaning of *elleltia* is
"to hinder" (VM, Nahuatl/Span., f. 28v).

²*Oquinqualancacuiti*: The normal form would be *oquinqualancuiti*. Molina gives the verb as *qualancuitia*, and in a series of related entries the incorporated element *qualanca-* predictably functions adverbially, not constituting an object as it does here.

³*Quitlahuellalilique*: this form appears at first glance to contain the root
tlahuel-, "bad, evil, wild," which would fit the context well, indicating that
the dependents put Juan Diego in a bad light with the bishop. Closer
analysis, however, shows that the *tla-* here must be an object prefix, so that
the basic verb is *huellalia*, "to correct or amend" (VM, Nahuatl/Span., f.

wooden bridge. Though they kept searching everywhere, no-where did they see him; they returned empty handed. Not only did they go away vexed because of the loss of time, but it frus-trated them[1] and made them angry. They went to tell the lord bishop about it, preparing him[3] not to believe him; they told him that he was only lying to him, only making up what he came to tell him, or that perhaps he only dreamed or saw in sleep walk-ing what he told him and asked of him. They insisted that if he should come again, should return, they would seize him on the spot and punish him severely, so that he would never lie and disturb people[4] again.

ON THE FOLLOWING day, Monday, Juan Diego did not return when he was supposed to take some sign in order to be be-lieved, because when he reached the home of an uncle of his, whose name was Juan Bernardino, a sickness had come upon him and he lay gravely ill. First he went to summon a physician for him, who looked after him for a while,[7] but it was too late; he was already mortally ill. When night had come his uncle asked him that while it was still very early in the morning and dark everywhere, he should come to Tlatelolco to summon one of the friars to go hear his confession and prepare him, because he was fully convinced that it was now time for him to die and that he would not rise again or recover.

IT WAS TUESDAY, still very dark everywhere, when Juan Diego left his home to summon a friar in Tlatelolco. When he came by the hill of Tepeyacac, at the foot of which the road that he took previously passes to the west, he said, "if I just go straight along the road, I am afraid that the Lady may see me, for before you

---

156). One could extrapolate, with the present word in its context, "they fixed it for him," or as we have hazarded, "prepared him." Despite the mor-phology, however, it is probable that Laso de la Vega's intention, following Miguel Sánchez (IVM, p. 85), was indeed "they made him look bad so that he would not be believed." See introduction, p. 12.

[4]*Tèquamanaz*: probably for *tequàmanaz* (*tequaàmanaz*).

[5]*Ìtla*: for *itlà*.

[6]*Ìtla*: probably for *itlà* (although according to Carochi "his uncle" is *itla* with a final long vowel and no glottal stop [AC, f. 2v]).

[7]*Oc ipan tlàto*; instead of "who looked after him a while," an alternate translation would make this phrase parallel to the one immediately preceding it, "[Juan Diego] first saw to it [getting a doctor for his uncle]."

nechmotzicalhuiz inic nichuiquiliz tlanezcayotl in teopixcatlàtohuani in yuh onechmonànahuatili; ma oc techcahua in tonete-
quipachol, ma oc nicnonochilìtihuetzi in teopixqui motolinia in
notlàtzin àmo ça quimochialìtoc. Niman ic contlacolhui in tepetl
itzallan ontlècoc ye nepa centlapal Tonatiuh yquiçayanpa quiçato
inic ìçiuhca açitiuh Mexico inic àmo quimotzicalhuiz in ilhuicac
Çihuapîlli in momati ca in ompa ic otlacolo ca àhuel quimottiliz,
in huel nohuiampa motztilìtica: Quittac quenin hualmotemohui
icpac in tepetzintli ompa hualmotztilìtoc in ompa yeppa con-
mottiliani,[1] conmonamiquilico in inacaztlan tepetl, conmoyaca-
tzacuililico, quimolhuili. Auh noxocoyouh, campa in tiyauh?
campa in titztiuh? Auh in yèhuatl cuix achi ic mellelmà? cuix
noçe pinahuac? cuix noçe ic mìçahui, momauhti? ixpantzinco
mopechtecac, quimotlàpalhui, quimolhuilì,

nochpochtzinè, noxocoyohuè, Çihuapillè ma ximopaquiltitie
quen otimixtonalti? cuix ticmohuelmachitia in motlaçònaca-
yotzin noTecuiyoè, nopiltzintzinè; nictequipachoz in mixtzin
in moyollòtzin, ma xicmomachiltitzino nochpochtzinè, ca
huellanauhtoc çe momaçehualtzin noTla huei cocoliztli in
itech omotlali ca yeppa ic momiquiliz, auh oc nonìçiuhtiuh in
mochantzinco Mexìco noconnonochiliz çeme in itlaçòhuan
toTecuiyo in toTeopixcahuã, conmoyolcuitilitiuh, ihuã con-
moçencahuilitiuh, canel yè inic otitlacatque, in ticchiaco in
tomiquiztequiuh. Auh intla onoconneltilito, ca niman nican
oc ceppa nihualnocuepaz, inic nonyaz noconitquiz, in mìì-
yotzin in motlàtoltzin Tlacatlè, Nochpochtzinè, ma xinech-
motlapopolhuili, ma oc ixquich ica xinechmopaccaìyohuilti
càmo ic nimitznoquelhuia,[2] noxocoyohuè, nopiltzintzinè, ca
niman moztla niquiztihuetziquiuh.

Auh in o yuh quimocaquiti itlàtol in Iuan Diego quimonanquilili
in icnohuàcaçenquizcaichpochtzintli:

Ma xiccaquì[3] ma huel yuh ye in moyollo noxocoyouh

---

[1] An equally grammatical solution, since the third person singular subjects and objects are not specified, would be "Watching from the top of the
hill where she had seen him before, she saw him coming down." Note,
however, that at the corresponding place (IVM, p. 87) Miguel Sánchez has
"descending from the hill where she was waiting for him, she came into his
path to meet him."

[2] *Càmo ic nimitznoquelhuia.* Just how the object prefix relates to the

know it she will detain me in order that I should carry the sign to the priestly ruler as she instructed me. May our affliction leave us first; let me first hurry to summon the friar. My uncle is in need and he can't just lie waiting for him." Thereupon he went around the hill, climbing through an opening and coming out on the other side to the east, so that he would quickly reach Mexico and the heavenly Lady would not detain him. He believed that if he went around there, she who sees absolutely everywhere would not be able to see him. He saw her coming down from the hill where she was watching, where he had seen her before.[1] She came to meet and intercept him on the hillside, saying to him, "Well, my youngest child, where are you going? Where are you headed?" And wasn't he a bit bothered by it? Or ashamed? Or startled and frightened by it? He prostrated himself before her, greeted her, and said to her,

My daughter, my youngest child, Lady, may you be content. How did you feel on awakening? Is your precious body in good health, my patron, my very noble lady? I am going to cause you concern. You must know, my daughter, that a poor subject of yours, my uncle, lies very gravely ill. A great illness has come upon him, of which he will soon die. And first I am hurrying to your home of Mexico to summon one of those beloved of our Lord, our friars, to go hear his confession and prepare him, for what we were born for is to come to await our duty of death. When I have carried this out, then I will return here again so that I may go to carry your message, O personage, my daughter. Please forgive me and meanwhile have patience with me. I am not doing it on purpose,[2] my youngest child, my very noble Lady. I will come by quickly tomorrow.

When she had heard Juan Diego's words, the compassionate, consummate Virgin answered him,

Understand, rest very much assured, my youngest child,

---

meaning is not clear; it is not elucidated in Molina's entry under "adrede dezir o hazer algo" (VM, Span./Nahuatl, f. 5). Possibly the sense is not "I am not doing it on purpose," but "I am not fooling you." See VM, Nahuatl/Span., f. 14, under "çanic tequeloani," and f. 89, under "quequeloa" and "quequelhuia."

[3]*Xiccaqui*: the final *i* is neither long nor followed by glottal stop.

macatle tlein mitzmauhti, mitztequipacho, macamo quen
mochihua in mix in moyollo, macamo xiquimacaci in cocoliztli, manoçe oc itlà cocoliztli cococ teòpouhqui, cuix àmo
nican nicà nimoNantzin? cuix àmo noçehuallotitlan, nècauh-
yotitlan in ticà? cuix àmo nèhuatl in nimopaccayeliz? cuix
àmo nocuixanco, nomamalhuazco in ticà? cuix oc itlà in motech monequì?[1] macamo oc itlà mitztequipacho, mitzàmana,
macamo mitztequipacho in icocoliz moTlàtzin càmo ic miquîz
in axcan itech ca; ma huel yuh ye in moyollo ca ye opàtic:
(Auh ca niman huel ìquac pàtic in iTlàtzin in iuh çatepan
machiztic.)
Auh in Iuan Diego in o yuh quicac in iìyotzin, in itlàtoltzin in
ilhuicac Çihuapilli, huel cenca ic omoyollali, huel ic pachiuh in
iyollo. Auh quimotlatlauhtili inic ma ça yè quimotitlanili inic
quittatiuh in Tlàtohuani Obispo in quitquiliz itlà inezca, in
ineltica, inic quineltocaz. Auh in ilhuicac Çihuapilli niman ic
quimonahuatilì, inic ontlècoz in icpac tepetzintli, in oncan canin
yeppa conmottiliaya; quimolhuili xitlèco noxocoyouh in icpac in
tepetzintli, auh in canin otinechittac, ihuan onimitznànahuati
oncan tiquittaz onoc nepapan xochitl, xictètequi, xicnechico,
xicçentlali, niman xichualtemohui, nican nixpan xichualhuica.
Auh in Iuan Diego niman ic quitlècahui in tepetzintli, auh in
oàcito icpac, çenca quimahuiçò in ixquich onoc, xotlatoc, cue-
pontoc in nepapan Caxtillan tlaçòxochitl, in ayamo imochiuhyan;
canel huel ìquac in motlàpaltilia izcetl: huel çenca àhuiaxtoc,
iuhqui in tlaçòepyollòtli inic yohualàhuachyòtoc; niman ic peuh
in quitètequi, huel moch quinechico, quicuixanten. Auh in oncan
icpac tepetzintli ca niman àtle xochitl in imochiuhyan, ca texcalla,
netzolla, huihuitztla, nòpalla, mizquitla; auh intla xiuhtotontin
mochichihuani in ìquac in ipan metztli Diziembre ca moch
quiquà,[2] quipòpolohua izçetl. Auh ca niman ic hualtemoc, qui-
hualmotquilili in ilhuicac Çihuapilli in nepapan xochitl oqui-
tètequito,

auh in o yuh quimottili imaticatzinco conmocuili; niman ye oc
çeppa icuexanco[3] quihualmotemili, quimolhuili,

---

[1]*Monequì*: the *i* is neither long nor followed by glottal stop.
[2]*Quiquà*: the *a* is neither long nor followed by glottal stop.

that nothing whatever should frighten you or worry you. Do not be concerned, do not fear the illness, or any other illness or calamity. Am I, your mother, not here? Are you not under my protective shade, my shadow? Am I not your happiness? Are you not in the security of my lapfold, in my carrying gear? Do you need something more? Do not let anything worry you or upset you further. Do not let your uncle's illness worry you, for he will not die of what he now has. Rest assured, for he has already recovered.

(And at that very moment his uncle recovered, as was learned afterwards.)

When Juan Diego heard the heavenly lady's message, he was greatly consoled and reassured by it. He implored her to send him to go see the lord bishop, taking him some sign or proof, so that he would believe him. Thereupon the heavenly Lady directed him to go up to the top of the hill where he had seen her before. She said to him, "Go up, my youngest child, to the top of the hill, and where you saw me and I spoke to you, you will see various kinds of flowers growing. Pick them, gather them, collect them, and then bring them back down here, bring them to me."

Then Juan Diego climbed the hill. When he reached the top, he was greatly astonished at all the different kinds of precious Spanish flowers that were growing there, blossoming and blooming, although their blooming time had not yet come, for it was right then that the frost was strong. They were very fragrant, and the night dew on them was like precious pearls. He thereupon began to pick them; he gathered every one and put them in his lapfold. But the top of the hill was absolutely no place for any flowers to grow, for it was a place of crags, thorns, brambles, cactus, and mesquite, and if some little grassy weeds should grow there at that time, in the month of December, the frost would devour and destroy them all. Then he came back down, bringing to the heavenly Lady the various kinds of flowers that he had gone to pick.

When she saw him, she took them in her arms; then she put them back in the folds of his cloak, saying to him,

---

[3]*Icuexanco*: *-cuexanco* is an older variant of the form *-cuixanco* which is mainly used in the text.

noxocoyouh inin nepapan xochitl yèhuatl in tlaneltiliz,[1] in nezcayotl in tichuiquiliz in Obispo, nopampa tiquilhuiz ma ic quitta in notlanequiliz, ihuã ic quineltiliz in notlanequiliz, in noçializ. Auh in tèhuatl in tinotitlan ca huel motech netlacaneconi; auh huel nimitztlaquauhnahuatia çan huel icel ixpan Obispo ticçohuaz in motilmà, ihuan ticnextiliz in tlein tichuica: auh huel moch ticpohuiliz, tiquilhuiz in quenin onimitznahuatì inic titlècoz in icpac tepetzintli in tictètequitiuh Xochitl, ihuã in ixquich otiquittac, oticmahuiçò, inic huel ticyollòyehuaz[2] in TeopixcaTlàtohuani; inic niman ipan tlàtoz înic mochihuaz, moquetzaz in noTeòcal oniquìtlanili.

Auh in ocõmonànahuatili in ilhuicac Çihuapilli quihualtocac in cuepòtli Mexìco huallamelahua, ye pactihuitz, ye yuh yetihuitz in iyollo ca yecquiçaquiuh, quiyecitquiz, huel quimocuitlahuìtihuitz in tlein icuixanco yetihuitz in manen itlà quimacauh, quimotlamachtìtihuitz in iàhuiaca in nepapan tlaçòxochitl.

In oàçico itecpanchan Obispo connamiquito in icalpixcauh, ihuan oc cequin itlannencahuan in tlàtocaTeopixqui, auh quintlatlauhti inic ma quimolhuilican in quenin quimottiliznequì;[3] yece ayac cemè quinec, àmo conmocaccanèque,[4] àço yè inic huel oc yohuatzinco; auh ànoce inic ye quiximatì, ça quintequipachoa inic imixtlan pilcatinemì,[5] yhuan ye oquinnonotzque in inicnihuã[6] in quipolotò in ìquac quitepotztocaque.

Huel huècauhtica in otlàtolchixticatca, auh in oquittaq ye huel huècauhtica in oncan ìcac motololtitìcac, tlatenmattìcac in àço notzaloz, ihuan in iuhquin mà itlà quihualitqui quicuixanotìcac; niman ye ic itech onàcique inic quittilizque tlein quihuicatz inic inyollo pachihuiz. Auh in oquittac in Iuan Diego ca niman àhuel quintlatiliz in tlein quihuicatz, ca ic quitolinizque, quitotopehuazque noçe ic quimictizque tepiton quihualnexti, ca xochitl; auh in yuh quittaque, ca moch Caxtillan nepapan xochitl, ihuan in càmo

---

[1]*Tlaneltiliz*: for *tlaneltiliztli*; compare *nezcayotl*.

[2]*Ticyollòyehuaz*: *yollòyehua* is a variant of *yolehua*.

[3]*Quimottiliznequì*: the final *i* is neither long nor followed by glottal stop.

[4]*Conmocacanèque*: for standard *conmocaccanecque*; perhaps the diacritic

My youngest child, these various kinds of flowers are the proof and the sign that you are to take to the bishop. You are to tell him on my behalf that thereby he should see my will and carry out my wish and my will, and that you, my messenger, are very trustworthy. I give you very strict orders to unfold your cloak only before the bishop and show him what you are carrying. You are to recount absolutely everything to him and tell him how I instructed you to climb to the top of the hill to pick the flowers, and everything that you saw and beheld, so that you may really inspire the priestly ruler to see to it immediately that my temple which I requested of him is built and raised.

When the heavenly Lady had given him the various instructions, he came following the causeway that leads directly here to Mexico. Now he came content, confident that it would turn out well, that he would carry it off. As he came he exercised great care with what he had in his lapfold, lest he drop anything, and he enjoyed the fragrance of the various kinds of precious flowers.

WHEN HE CAME to the bishop's palace, the majordomo and other dependents of the priestly ruler went out to meet him, and he asked them to tell him that he wished to see him. But none of them wanted to; they pretended not to hear him, perhaps because it was still very early in the morning or perhaps because they now recognized him, that he would just annoy them with his hanging around in front of them; their friends who lost him when they were following after him had already cautioned them.

He was waiting for a reply for a very long time. When they saw that he had stood there for a very long time with his head down, that he was doing nothing in case he was called, and it seemed as if he came carrying something that he was keeping in his lapfold, they approached him to see what he came carrying, to satisfy their curiosity. And when Juan Diego saw that he could by no means hide from them what he came carrying and that because of it they would pester him, shove him, or maybe

---

was intended for the final *e*, which is followed by glottal stop. Conceivably the diacritic represents the weakening of the first of two [k]'s to glottal stop. The same thing may have happened at n. 4, pp. 98–99.

[5]*Pilcatinemi*: the final *i* is neither long nor followed by glottal stop.

[6]*Inicnihuan*: for *imicnihuan*.

imochiuhyan in ìquac, huel cenca quimahuiçòque; ihuan in quenin huel cenca çeltic inic cueponqui, inic àhuiyac, inic mahuiztic:
auh quelèhuique[1] inic quezquitetl conanazq̃, quiquixtilizque; auh
huel expa mochiuhq̃ inic motlàpalòque concuizquia; niman àhuel
mochiuhq̃, yèica in ìquac quiquitzquizquia[2] aocmo huel xochitl
in quittaya çan iuhquî mà tlàcuilolli, noce tlàmachtli, noce tlà-
tzontli in itech quittaya Tilmàtli.

Niman ic quimolhuilito in Tlàtohuani Obispo, in tlein oquittaque,
ihuan in quenin quimottiliznequi in maçehualtzintli ye izquipa
huallalauh,[3] ihuan in ye huel huècauh in ye icoço[4] oncà tlatlà-
tolchixtoc, inic quimottiliznequi. Auh in Tlàtohuani Obispo in o
yuh quimocaquiti niman ipan ya in iyollotzin ca yèhuatl in ineltica inic iyollotzin màciz, inic quimoneltililiz in tlein ic nemì[5] tlacatzintli: niman motlanahuatili inic niman calaquiz, quimottiliz;

auh in ocalac ixpantzinco mopechtecac in iuh yeppa quichihuani;
auh oc ceppa quimotlapohuililì[6] in ixquich oquittac, in oquimahuiçò, ihuan in inetitlaniz: quimolhuili
    Notecuiyoè Tlàtohuaniè ca ye onicchiuh, ca ye onicneltilì in
yuh otinechmonahuatilì, ca huel yuh onicnolhuilito in tlacatl
in noTecuiyo in ilhuicac Çihuapilli Santa MARIA in Teotl
Dios itlaçònantzin, in ticmìtlania in tlanezcayotl inic huel ti-
nechmoneltoquitiz, inic ticmochihuililiz in iTeòcaltzin in
oncan mitzmìtlanililia, ticmoquechiliz; auh ca huel yuh
onicnolhuili, in onimitznomaquili in notlàtol inic nimitzhual-
nohuiquililiz in itlà inezca in ineltica in itlanequiliztzin inic
nomac oticmocahuili. Auh ca oquimohuelcaquiti in miì-
yotzin, in motlàtoltzin; auh oquimopaccaçelili in ticmìtlania,

---

[1]*Quelèhuique*: the *e* bearing the grave accent is long, not followed by
glottal stop.
[2]*Quiquitzquizquia*: *quitzquia* is equivalent to *tzitzquia*; see Lockhart
1992, p. 588, n. 13, line 4.
[3]*Huallalauh*: this seems to be an inadvertent combination of *hualla*, the
preterit, and *huallauh*, the present of the verb "to come."
[4]*Icoço*: an apparently garbled form we have been unable to decipher; it
probably represents another term meaning a long time, like the one just
preceding.

beat him, he showed them by a little glimpse that it was flowers. When they saw that there were all different kinds of Spanish flowers and that they were not in season at that time, they marveled greatly at it and at how very fresh they were, like just opened flowers, pleasant to smell, splendid. They wanted to seize a few of them and take them from him. But all three times when they tried to step forward to take them, they were entirely unsuccessful, because when they were about to grasp[2] them, it was no longer real flowers that they saw but something seemingly painted, embroidered, or sewn on the cloak.

Thereupon they went to tell the lord bishop what they had seen and how the humble commoner who had come several times was wanting to see him and that now he had been waiting there for a very long time[4] for word about his wanting to see him. When the lord bishop heard this, it came to him that it was the proof that would convince him to carry out what the humble person was after. Then he gave orders that he should enter immediately and that he would see him.

And when he entered, he prostrated himself before him, as he had done before, and again he told him all that he had seen and beheld and his mission. He said to him:

My lord ruler, now I have done and carried out what you ordered me. Indeed I went to tell the lady my patron, the heavenly Lady, Saint Mary, the precious mother of God the deity, that you asked for a sign so that you can believe me and build her temple for her in the place where she asks you to erect it. I assured her that I gave you my word that I would bring back to you some sign and verification of her wish, since you left it in my hands. She approved your message, and she gladly accepted your request for some sign, some verification of it, so that her will may be performed

---

[5]*Nemi*: the *i* is neither long nor followed by glottal stop.

[6]*Quimotlapohuilili*. This form is correct in itself, but by strictest grammar it is not correct in context. The root verb *pohua*, "to tell," etc., here has the indefinite object *tla* despite the fact that specific direct objects follow outside the verb (*in ixquich oquittac*, "all he saw," and others). Nevertheless, the native-speaker Nahuatl of the time did occasionally seem to specify objects after the indefinite object prefix, and with some verbs, for some speakers, the *tla-* became so incorporated into the stem as no longer to serve its normal function.

in itlà inezca ìneltica[1] inic mochihuaz, moneltiliz in itlanequiliztzin: auh yè in in axcan oc yohuatzinco onechmo-
nahuatili inic oc ceppa nimitznottiliquiuh; auh onicnìtlanilili
in itlà inezca inic nineltocoz, in yuh onechmolhuili nech-
momaquiliz; auh ca çan niman oquimoneltilili,

auh onechmihuali in icpac tepetzintli in canin yeppa nocon-
nottiliani inic ompa nictètequitiuh in nepapan Caxtillan
xochitl: auh in onictequitò,[2] onichualnohuiquilili in oncan
tlatzintlan; auh ca imaticatzinco conmocuili, oc ceppa nocuixanco oconhualmotemili inic nimitzhualnotquililiz, in huel
tèhuatzin nimitznomaquiliz maçihui in ca huel nicmatia càmo
imochiuhyã xochitl in icpac tepetzintli, ca çan tètexcalla,
netzolla, huitztlà tenòpalla, mizquitlà àmo ic oninotzotzon,
àmo ic nomeyolloac

in nàcito in icpac tepetzintli in nitlachix ca ye xochitlalpan,
oncan cenquiztoc in ixquich nepapã tlaçòxochitl in Caxtillancayotl àhuachtonameyòtoc inic niman onictètequito. Auh
onechmolhuili inic ipampa nimitznomaquiliz; auh ca ye yuh
nicneltilia inic oncan ticmottiliz in itlà nezcayotl in ticmì-
tlanilia, inic ticmoneltililiz in itlanequiliztzin; ihuan inic neci
ca neltiliztli in notlàtol, in nonetitlaniz: ca iz ca ma xicmo-
celili;

auh ca niman ic quihualçouh in iztac itilmà ic oquicuixanotìcaca
xochitl; auh in yuh hualtepeuh in ixquich nepapan Caxtillan
xochitl, niman oncan momachioti, neztiquiz in itlaçòixiptlatzin
izçenquizcaichpochtli Santa MARIA Teotl Dios Inantzin in
yuhcatzintli axcan moyetztica in oncan axcan mopixtzinotica in
itlaçòchantzinco in iTeòcaltzinco Tepeyacac motocayotia Guadalupe.

Auh in o yuh quimottili in Tlàtohuani Obispo, ihuan in ixquichtin oncan catca motlanquaquetzque çenca quimahuiçòq̃, quimo-
tztimoquetzque, tlaocoxquè, moyoltoneuhquè, yuhquin àco yà in
inyollo in intlalnamiquiliz: auh in tlàtohuani Obispo choquiztica,
tlaocoyaliztica quimotlatlauhtili, quimìtlanilili in itlapopolhuililoca, inic àmo niman oquineltili, in itlanequiliztzin in ìiyotzin in
itlàtoltzin.

---

[1]*Ìneltica*: the first *i* is long, not followed by glottal stop. The word in
question is (in the possessed form) *nelticayotl*, a patientive deverbal noun
from *nelti*, here in the sense "to be verified."

and carried out. Well, then, today, while it was still very early in the morning, she instructed me to come to see you again. I asked her for some sign of it so that I would be believed, as she said that she would give me, and right then she carried it out.

She sent me to the top of the hill where I had seen her before to go cut various kinds of Spanish flowers. When I had cut them, I brought them back to her down there below. She took them in her arms, then put them back in the folds of my cloak in order that I might bring them back to you and give them to you in person. Although I fully realized that the top of the hill is not a place where flowers grow, that it is only a place of crags, thorns, brambles, cactus, and mesquite, I did not for that reason have any doubts.

When I reached the top of the hill and looked about, it was a flower garden, full of all different kinds of fine flowers in the Spanish style, glistening with dew, so that I immediately went to pick them. And she told me that I was to give them to you on her behalf. Thus I am carrying it out, so that in them you may see what you request as a sign to carry out her wish, and it will be seen that my message and my errand are true. Here they are, please accept them.

Thereupon he spread out his white cloak, in the folds of which he was carrying the flowers, and as all the different kinds of Spanish flowers scattered to the ground, the precious image of the consummate Virgin Saint Mary, mother of God the deity, was imprinted and appeared on the cloak, just as it is today where it is kept in her precious home, her temple of Tepeyacac, called Guadalupe.

When the lord bishop and all who were there saw it, they knelt down, they marveled greatly at it, they looked at it transfixed, they grieved, their hearts were afflicted; it was as if their spirits and their minds were transported upward. The lord bishop, with tears and sorrow, implored and asked her forgiveness for not having immediately carried out her wish, her message.

---

[2]*Onictequitò*: the final vowel is neither long nor followed by glottal stop.

Auh in omoquetz, quihualton in iquechtlan ic ilpiticatca in itla-
quen in itilmà Iuan Diego in itech omonexiti in oncan omomachiotìtzino in ilhuicac Çihuapilli. Auh niman ic quimohuiquili,
ompa quimotlalilito in ineteochihuayan:
auh oc oncã oçemilhuiti in Iuan Diego in ichantzinco Obispo oc
quimotzicalhui, auh in imoztlayoc quilhuì çaque[1] inic ticteìttitiz[2]
in canin itlanequiliztzin ilhuicac Çihuapilli quimoquechililizque in
iTeòcaltzin: niman ic tetlalhuiloc inic mochihuaz moquetzaz.

Auh in Iuan Diego in o yuh quiteittiti in canin quimonahuatilì
ilhuicac Çihuapilli moquetzaz iTeòcaltzin nimã ic tenahuati in oc
onàciznequi in ichan inic conittatiuh in iTlàtzin Iuan Bernardino
in huellanauhtoc in ìquac quihualcauhtehuac çeme quinotzazquia
Teopixque in oncã Tlatilolco inic quiyolcuitizquia, quiçencahuazquia; in quimolhuili ilhuicac Çihuapilli in ye opàtic.
Auh àmo çan içel quicauhque yaz, ca quihuicaque in ompa in i-
chan; auh in o yuh àçito quittaque in iTlàtzin ye huel pactica
niman àtle quicocoa, auh in yèhuatl cenca quimahuiçò in quenin
imach hualhuico, ihuan çenca mahuiztililo, quitlàtlani in imach
tleica in yuhqui chihualo, in çenca mahuiztililo: auh in yèhuatl
quilhuì in quenin ìquac ompa hualehuac in quinochilizquia teopixqui in quiyolcuitiz, quiçencahuaz; in oncan tepeyacac quimottilitzino in ilhuicac Çihuapilli; auh quimotitlani in ompa Mexico in quittatiuh in tlàtohuani Obispo inic oncã quimocaltiliz in
tepeyacac. Auh quimolhuili in macamo motequipachò[3] in ca ye
pactica; inic çenca moyollali:
quilhui in iTlàtzin ca ye nelli ca nimã ìquac in quimopàtili, yhuã
huel quimottili izçanno huel ye iuhcatzintli in iuh quimot-
titìtzinoaya in iMach; ihuan quimolhuilì in quenin yèhuatl oc
oquimotitlanili Mexìco in quittaz Obispo. Auh ma no in ìquac
yèhuatl quittatiuh[4] ma huel moch ic quixpãtiz quinonotzaz in tlein
oquittac, ihuan in quenin tlamahuiçoltica oquimopàtili: auh ma
huel yuh quimotocayotiliz, ma huel yuh motocayotitzinoz izçenquizcaichpochtzintli Santa M A R I A de Guadalupe in

---

[1]*Çaque*: A hortatory particle consisting of *ça*, "just," and *oque* (*oc è* =
yè), the particle proper. Though not elsewhere attested in just this form, it
fits well into the family of variants of *oque* given by Molina under "Ea"
(VM, Span./ Nahuatl, f. 48), in more than one of which the *o* is elided after
a preceding *a*. Molina's list: "tlaq̃. tlaoque. oque. maque. maoque."
[2]*Ticteìttitiz*: the *i* with diacritic is neither long nor followed by glottal

When he arose, he loosened the garment which was tied around Juan Diego's neck, his cloak, on which the heavenly Lady had appeared, on which she had imprinted herself. Thereupon he took it to place it in his oratory.

Juan Diego stayed one more day in the bishop's palace, he detained him for a while. The following day he said to him, "Let us go[1] so that you may show people the place where it is the heavenly Lady's wish that they build a temple for her." Thereupon orders were given for it to be built and erected.

After Juan Diego had shown where the heavenly Lady instructed that her temple be erected, he took his leave, because he wanted to go home to see his uncle, Juan Bernardino, who lay gravely ill when he left him behind to summon one of the friars in Tlatelolco to hear his confession and prepare him, and who the heavenly Lady told him had already recovered.

But they did not let him go alone. They accompanied him to his home, and when he arrived they saw that his uncle was now entirely healthy, that nothing whatever ailed him. And he was greatly astonished at how his nephew came accompanied and was rendered great honor, and he asked his nephew how it happened that he was thus greatly honored. He told him how when he left to call the friar to hear his confession and prepare him, the heavenly Lady appeared to him at Tepeyacac and sent him to Mexico to go see the lord bishop so that he would build her a house in Tepeyacac and how she told him not to worry, since he was already well, by which he had been greatly consoled.

His uncle told him that it was the truth, that she cured him at that very moment, and that he really saw her in exactly the same way as she appeared to his nephew, and that she told him that meanwhile she was sending him to Mexico to see the bishop. He [the uncle] was then to go see him too, he was to put absolutely everything before him, he was to inform him of what he had seen and how she had healed him miraculously, and that he was to give her precious image the very name of the consum-

---

stop. Possibly the word was confused with *itoa*, "to say" (often written *ittoa* in the present text).

[3]*Motequipachò*: the final *o* is neither long nor followed by glottal stop.

[4]*Quittatiuh*. According to Carochi, this form should be *quittà* or *quittati*. See pp. 66–67, n. 4.

itlaçòixiptlatzin.

Auh niman ic quihualhuicaque in Iuan Bernardino in ixpan Tlàtohuani Obispo in quinonotzaco, in ixpan tlaneltilico. Auh inehuan in imach Iuan Diego quincalloti in ichan Obispo achi
quezquilhuitl in oc ixquich ica moquetzinò[1] iTeòcaltzin tlàtoca-
Çihuapilli in oncan Tepeyacac in canin quimottitili in Iuan Diego.
Auh in tlàtohuani Obispo quìquani ompa in Iglesia Mayor in
itlaçòIxiptlatzin in ilhuicac tlaçòÇihuapilli, quihualmoquixtili in
ompa itecpanchan, in ineteochihuayan moyetzticatca; inic mochi
tlacatl quittaz, quimahuiçoz in itlaçòIxiptlatzin.
Auh huel çenmochi izçemaltepetl olin, in quihualmottiliaya, in
quimahuiçoaya in itlaçòixiptlatzin, huallateomatia, quimotlatlauhtiliaya; çenca quimahuiçoaya in quenin teotlamahuiçoltica inic
omonexiti, inic nimã mà aca[2] tlalticpac tlacatl oquimìcuilhui in
itlaçòixiptlayotzin.

In tilmàtzintli ineolol catca in Iuan Diego in itech tlamahuiçoltica monexiti in ixiptlatzin ilhuicac Çihuapilli ca Ayatzintli achi
tilactic catca, ihuan tlayecìquitilli yèica ca in ìquac in, in maçehualtzitzintin mochtin ayatl in intlaquen in inNeololtzin catca,
Çan yèhuantin in Pipiltin in Teteuctin, yhuan in yaotiàcahuan in
yamanqui in ichcatilmàtli ic mochìchihuaya, ic mololoaya: in
ayatl ca ye momati ichtli ic mochihua, in itech quiça in metl: auh
inin tlaçòayatzintli in itech monexiti in çenquizcaichpochtzintli
toçihuapillatòcatzin ca ozçotitica yamancaicpatl inic ìtzontica, inic
çaliuhtica; auh inic quauhtic in itlaçòixiptlayotzin in itech ompe-
hua in ixocpaltzin inic onàci iquayollotzinco quipia chiquacem-
iztitl[3] ihuan çe çihuaiztitl;
in itlaçòxayacatzin çenquizca mahuiztic, tecpiltic acìi yayactic, in
itlaçòtlactzin inic monexitia mocnomatcatzintli, îelpantzinco mo-
manepanotzinotìcac, oncan hualpeuhtica in ipitzahuayantzinco:
auh camòpaltic in inelpiayatzin; çaniyo in yeccampa icxitzin
tepiton iquac neci in icactzin nextic: in inechìchihualtzin tlaztale-

---

[1]*Moquetzinò*: another case of *tz* for *tztz*, as at n. 7, pp. 62–63, and involving the same roots.

[2]*Nimã mà aca.* This phrase appears to need some word such as *ayac*, "no
one," after *nimã* in order to be complete. *Niman* and *mà acà* normally

mate Virgin, Saint Mary of Guadalupe, that it was to bear that very name.

Thereupon they brought Juan Bernardino before the lord bishop to inform him and verify it in his presence. The bishop lodged the two of them, him and his nephew Juan Diego, in his palace for quite a few days until such time as the temple of the Queen was erected at Tepeyacac where she appeared to Juan Diego. The lord bishop moved the precious image of the heavenly precious Lady to the cathedral; he removed it from his palace, where it had been in his oratory, so that everyone would see and marvel at her precious image.

There was a movement in all the altepetls everywhere of people coming to see and marvel at her precious image. They came to show their devotion and pray to her; they marveled greatly at how it was by a divine miracle that she had appeared, that absolutely no earthly person[2] had painted her precious image.

THE CLOAK on which the image of the heavenly Lady miraculously appeared was the garment of Juan Diego, a maguey cloak that was rather thick and well woven, for at that time the maguey cloak was the clothing and covering of all the humble commoners. Only those who were nobles, lords, and prominent warriors adorned and wrapped themselves in cloaks of soft cotton. This type of cloak, as is well known, is made of fiber that comes from the maguey. This precious cloak on which the consummate Virgin, our Queen, appeared, is of two quarter-lengths, sewn together and fastened with soft thread. Her precious image is six spans[3] and a woman's span high from the bottom of her foot to the crown of her head.

Her precious face, which is perfectly wondrous, is courtly and somewhat dark; her precious torso is such that she appears to be a person of humility; she stands with her hands joined together at the breast, beginning at her waist; her belt is purple; only the tip of her right foot shows a bit; her shoe is gray. On

intensify negative statements, but do not constitute such in and of themselves.

[3]*Iztitl: jeme* or span, the distance between the extended thumb and index finger.

hualtic inic neçi panipa;[1] auh in içeçehuallopan iuhquin chichiltic, inic nepapan xochitlàtlamàcho,[2] izquixochimimìnqui:[3] auh nohuiã teocuitlatene; auh inic motzitzquìtica in iquechtlantzinco teocuitlayahualli tlilhuahuanqui inic tenmalacachiuhtica, inepantla cà Cruz. Auh oc no tlàtecpa hualneci oc no çe itlaquentzin yamanqui iztac huel imàquechtlantzinco hualàaçitica, tenchayahuac. Auh in pani itlapachiuhcatzin ilhuicaxoxiuhqui, huel iquapantzinco onhualehua,[4] àtle ic quitlapachoa in ixayacatzin, huel icxitlantzinco hualhuetzi achi nepantlà ic màpantzinotica: huel nohuian teocuitlatene, achi patlactic inic tene; auh nohuian teocuitlaçiçitlallo: auh in ye mochintin çiçitlaltin ompohualtin onchiquaçẽteme.

Auh in itzontecontzin yc iyeccanpantzinco[5] inic motololtitìcac; auh icpantzinco[6] manì[7] teocuitlacorona quaquahuitztic ipan in itlapachiuhcatzin. Auh icxitlantzinco ca in metztli tlacpacpa in itztìcac in iquaquauh, huel inepantlà in moquetzinòticac, auh no yuh neci huel no inepantlà in tonatiuh inic quimotoquilitìcac in itonameyo nohuiampa quimoyahualhuìticac, huel macuilpoalli in iteocuitlapepetlaquillo, çequi huehueyac, cequi tepitoton, ihuan cuecuetlanqui. Auh huel màtlactin omome in quiyahualoa in ixayacatzin, ihuan in itzontecontzin, auh in ye mochi nenecoc ic huetzì[8] ompohualli onmàtlactli in itonameyotzin, in ipepetlaquillotzin; auh in itlòtloc inic tlatlantica iten tilmàtli iztac mextli[9] in quimoyahualhuitìcac.

Auh inin ytlaçòixiptlatzin ihuan in ye mochi ca çe Angel in ipan tlacçatìcac, çan huel ipitzahuayan tlantica inic neçi; auh in icxitlãpa àtle neçi yuhquin mixtitlan actica; inic ontlami in itẽ tilmàtli itlapachiuhcatzin ilhuicac Çihuapilli, in icxitlampatzinco huel yectli inic onhuehuetzi nohuian necoccampa quitzìtzitzquitìcac Angel; auh in ineololol, in inechìchiuh chichiltic, auh teocuitlatl

---

[1]*Panipa*: the reference may be to the outer garment as opposed to the inner one mentioned below.

[2]*Xochitlàtlamàcho*: the last of the *a*'s is not followed by glottal stop. The intention may have been *xochitlàtlàmacho* (though the text never marks glottal stops in consecutive syllables) or, more likely, *xochitlàtlamachò*.

[3]*Izquixochimimìnqui*: for *izquixochimìminqui*. *Izquitl*, "popcorn," refers to various white flowers in clusters (see DK, p. 123).

[4]*Onhualehua*: *onehua* has among others the meaning "to fit correctly" (VM, Nahuatl/Span., f. 77). Unless the *on-* is connected with the verb lexically, the simultaneous presence of directional prefixes indicating opposite directions is a rarity indeed. Yet *onehua* can also mean "to leave, de-

the surface,[1] her outfit appears to be rose colored, and in the shadowy parts, it almost seems crimson, embroidered with various kinds of flowers, darted with popcorn flowers;[3] and it has gold edges all around. It is fixed at her neck by a gold disk, with a black outline going around its border; in the middle of it is a cross. And also there appears on the inside another garment of hers, soft and white; it reaches all the way to her wrists; the edge is unraveled. On top, her sky blue veil rests snugly on her head,[4] not covering her face in any way. It falls all the way to her feet, gathered together somewhat at the middle, with gold edges all around, which are somewhat wide, and it is speckled all over with gold stars; the stars total forty-six.

Her head is bent to her right, and on her head, on top of her veil is a golden crown, [its peaks] narrower at the top, wider at the bottom. At her feet is the moon, its horns facing upward; she stands right in the middle of it. She also appears to be right in the middle of the sun, so that its rays follow her and surround her on all sides; there are exactly one hundred golden rays, some long, some very short, and they shine brightly. Exactly twelve surround her face and head, and her rays or beams falling on both sides total fifty. Near where the edge of the cloak ends is a white cloud which surrounds it.

This precious image of hers and all the rest stand on an angel, who appears to come to an end right at his waist. Toward his feet nothing appears, as if he enters the cloud, because the edge of the cloak ends there. Everywhere on both sides the angel is holding the heavenly Lady's veil, which falls gracefully to her feet. His clothing, his adornment, is bright red, and the fasten-

---

part." An alternate translation might be "[her veil] comes straight down from her head, not covering . . ."

[5]*Iyeccanpantzinco*: for *iyeccanpatzinco*.

[6]*Icpantzinco*: for *icpactzinco*.

[7]*Mani*: the *i* is neither long nor followed by glottal stop.

[8]*Huetzi*: the *i* is neither long nor followed by a glottal stop, unless a plural is intended. The rays are mainly (though not entirely) treated as grammatically singular here, and in any case the text rarely indicates the glottal stop of verbal plurals.

[9]*Mextli*: standard *mixtli*.

in iquechtlan ic çaliuhtica; auh in iAtlapal nepapan quetzalli, nepapan ìhuitl çoçouhtìcac,[1] quihuicatìcac in imàma Angel; auh inic
neçi huel iuhqui in pactìcac motlamachtitìcac inic quimo-
napalhuìtica in ilhuicac Tlàtocaçihuapilli. —

NICAN MOTECPANA
IN IXQVICH TLAMAHVIÇOLLI YE QVIMO-
CHIHVILIA IN ILHVICAC ÇIHVAPILLI
TOTLAÇONANTZIN GVADALVPE.
(†)

HVel quiyacatì in ìquac yancuican quimohuiquilìque in ompa
tepeyacac in o yuh yecauh in iteòcaltzin, in ixquich tlamahuiçolli
quimochihuili. Ca in ìquac in, ca huel mohueychiuh in tlayahualoliztli ic quimohuiquilique, çenquizque in ixquichtin teopixque
catca ihuan in nepapan Caxtilteca in ye inmac catca altepetl; no
ihuan in ixquichtin Tlàtoque Pipiltin Mexìca; ihuan in oc çequin
nohuian altepehuàcan tlaca, huel tlaçencahualoc, inic yectlachì-
chihualoc in nohuian ipan Cuepòtli inic hualquiztica Mexìco inic
onàci Tepeyacac in oncã omoquetz iTeocaltzin in ilhuicac Çihuapilli. Huel miec inic oneahuiltiloc, inic pàpacoac, inic huiloac; in
cuepòtli huel tentihuia, ihuan in necoccampa atezcatl ca huel oc
huècatlan catca àmo çan quexquich in maçehualli acalco huia
cequin mìcalìtihuia, moyaonanamiquia. Çeme yèhuan in tlamin-
què in moChichimecachìchihuaya, achi huel contilini in itlahuìtol,[2] auh àmo inèmachpan quiztiquiz in mitl niman quimin
çeme in oncan mìcaltinenca quinalquixti in iquech niman oncan
huetz: auh in oquittaque ca ye omomiquilì niman quimohui-
quililìque izcenquizcaIchpochtli toçihuapillatòcatzin ixpantzinco
quitecatò, in ihuayolque[3] quimotzàtzililia inic ma tlacahua yn
iyollotzin, ma quimozcalili, Auh in o yuh quihualcopinilìque in
mitl, àmo çaniyo in quimozcalili, in quimoyolitili, no ihuan nimã
pàtic in oncan ic nalquiz in mitl, ça ixquich mocauhtiquiz in
inezca, inic calac, ihuan inic quiz in mitl: auh niman moquetz-

---

[1]*Çoçouhtìcac*. This form implies an unattested intransitive cognate of
transitive *çohua/çoçohua* (see VM, Nahuatl/Span., ff. 24v–25).
[2]*Itlahuìtol*: the *i* marked with a grave accent is long and not followed by
a glottal stop.

ing at his neck is gold; his wings, of various kinds of rich plumes and other feathers, are spread out, and the angel's arms are parallel to them. As it appears, he is very happy and enjoys carrying the heavenly Queen in his arms.

HERE IS AN ORDERED ACCOUNT
OF ALL THE MIRACLES
THAT THE HEAVENLY LADY, OUR PRECIOUS MOTHER
OF GUADALUPE, HAS PERFORMED.
(†)

THE VERY FIRST of the miracles that she worked was when they took her to Tepeyacac for the first time after her temple was finished. For at this time the procession in which they took her was performed in the grand fashion. All the priests that there were, and the various Spaniards in whose hands the city was, and also all the Mexica rulers and nobles, came out together, as well as the people from other altepetls all around. Great preparations were made so that things would be well adorned all along the causeway which leaves Mexico as far as Tepeyacac, where the temple of the heavenly Lady had been erected. There were many things for amusement and celebration along the way. The causeway was full of moving people, and since the water of the lake was still very deep on both sides, numerous commoners went by boat; some went along skirmishing, encountering one another in battle. One of the archers who were dressed like Chichimeca drew his bow quite taut, and without warning the arrow flew off and hit one of those who were engaged in skirmishing there; it passed through his neck, and he fell. When they saw that he had died, they took him to the consummate Virgin our Queen; they went and laid him before her. His relatives cried out to her to deign to revive him. And after they pulled the arrow out of him, she not only revived him and gave him life, but he was also immediately healed where the arrow

---

[3]*Ihuayolque*: standard *ihuanyolque*, with the *n* used elsewhere in the text (though this *n* was in fact often omitted, even by writers close to the Spanish orthographic tradition).

tehuac, còtlatocti inic quimopàpaquiltiliaya in ilhuicac Çihuapilli;
auh huel mochi tlacatl çenca tlamahuiçò; ihuan quimoyectenehuilìque izçenquizcaichpochtli ilhuicac Çihuapilli Santa MARIA
de Guadalupe; in quenin ye quimoneltililìtiuh in itlàtoltzin in
quimolhuili in Iuan Diego, inic çemìcac quinmopalehuiliz, quinmomanahuiliz in nican tlaca; ihuan in aquìque itechtzinco motza-
tzilizque. Auh yuh mìttoa inin tlacatzintli niman ìquac oncan
mocauh in itlaçòchantzinco in ilhuicac Tlaçòçihuapilli oncan qui-
motlàtlachpaniliaya in iteòcaltzin, in ithualtzin in iquiahuactzin.[1]

IN ìquac huey cocoliztli manca in ipan xihuitl mill y quinientos y
quarenta y quatro, in huellalpoliuh in ipã huèhuey Altepetl,
çeçemilhuitl motocaya macuilpohualli Tlacatl nel conpanahuiaya;
in o yuh quimottilìque in itlaçòhuan totecuiyo San Francisco Teopixque in àmo çehui, in niman àtle quimopàchihuia, in ye ahuil[2]
òtlatoca, in ye motlalcanahuilia, in ye motlalpolhuia in ipalnemo-
ani toTecuiyo; niman ipan motlàtoltìque inic tlayahualoloz,
huiloaz in ompa Tepeyacac, in tlaçòTeopixque quinmonechi-
calhuìque huel miactin in pipiltzitzintin, çihua, oquichtin in quin
ye chiquacenxiuhtia, in quin ye chiconxiuhtia momecahui-
tectàque[3] inic yà tlayahualoliztli: oncan hualquiz in Tlatelolco
Teopan, çemòtlica quimotzatzililitàque in toTecuiyo inic ma
quimocnoyttili in iatzin, in itepetzin, ma ye ixquich in içomaltzin,
in iqualantzin, ma çã huel icatzinco, ipãpatzinco in itlaçòmahuizNantzin izçẽquizcaichpochtli, toçihuapillatòcatzin Santa
M A R I A de Guadalupe Tepeyacac: huel yuh àçito in iTeo-
pãChantzinco in ompa huel miec tlatlatlauhtiliztli quimochi-
huilìque in Teopixque. Auh quimonequilti in ipalnemohuani

---

[1]*Iquiahuactzin. Ithualli quiahuatl* (patio and exit) is a metaphor for home
or household. By conventional grammar the possessed reverential form of
quiahuatl should be *-quiahuatzin.* The word was used so much in the
locative, however, with the relational word *-c* ("in, at," etc.) that here the *c*
has been incorporated into the noun stem. It is no longer conceived as a
relational word, for in that case the ending would be *-tzinco*; note that the
parallel nouns are in the simple possessed form. Actually, in our experience,
Nahuatl idiom calls not for a direct object with *tlachpana,* "to sweep," but
for a noun in the locative, for the *tla-* of *tlachpana* is the indefinite object,
rendering the verb intransitive.

[2]*Ahuil*: probably for *ahuel,* "impossible." *Ahuel òtlatoca* would be "it

had passed through; all that remained were marks where the arrow entered and came out. Right away he stood up and left; the heavenly Lady sent him on his way, making him joyful. Absolutely everyone marveled greatly and praised the consummate Virgin, the heavenly Lady, Saint Mary of Guadalupe, for the way she was now carrying out the pledge she made to Juan Diego that she would always help and defend the local people and all those who invoked her. It is said that from that moment on this humble person remained at the precious home of the heavenly precious Lady; there he used to sweep her temple and home for her.

WHEN THERE WAS a great epidemic in the year 1544, with very severe loss in the great altepetls, each day a hundred people were being buried; in truth, it exceeded that. When our Lord's precious ones, the friars of Saint Francis, had seen that it was not subsiding, that nothing at all was helping, that no progress could be made,[2] that our Lord the giver of life was reducing and depopulating the land, they arranged a procession to go to Tepeyacac. The precious friars gathered a great many children, female and male, who had just reached the age of six or seven; they went along flogging themselves.[3] As to how the procession went, it came out of the church at Tlatelolco; all along the way, they went crying to our Lord to have pity on his altepetl, that there be an end to his ire and wrath, in the very name and for the sake of his precious, revered mother, the consummate Virgin, our Queen, Saint Mary of Guadalupe of Tepeyacac. As soon as they arrived at her churchly home, the friars offered very many prayers. And God the giver of life willed that through the intercession and prayers of the compassionate personage, his

---

cannot go forward." This interpretation suffers from unclarity as to what the subject is, but it seems preferable to the other possibilities. Velázquez (HT, p. 106, n. 211) posits an intention *ahuic*, which would give "it goes from side to side (stumbles, sways, or wanders)." Conceivably, however, the printed original is correct. There is in fact an *ahuil-* which can be prefixed to verb and noun stems, adding, usually, the notion "in vain." The expression would then be written *ahuilòtlatoca*, and the translation might be "it was going badly." The problem with the subject remains, and like Velázquez we are reluctant to believe that *ahuil-* combines well with *òtlatoca*.

[3]Penitential processions involving children were common in fifteenth- and sixteenth-century Spain. See Christian 1981, pp. 217–18.

Dios in ica itepantlàtoltzin,[1] in itlatlatlauhtiliztzin in icnohuàcatzintli, in itlaçòmahuiznantzin niman çeuhta in cocoliztli, in
imoztlayoc,[2] aocmo miac tlacatl in omotocac; yequene ça cana
ome, yei tlacatl inic çehuito cocoliztli.

IN oc ipeuhyan in quin iuh hualàçico tlaneltoquiliztli, in nican
tlalpan in axcan motocayotia Nueua España; huel cenca miac inic
quinmotlaçòtili, inic quinmopalehuili, inic quinmomanahuili in
ilhuicac Çihuapilli çenquizcaichpochtli Santa MARIA in nican
tlaca inic huel quimomacazque, in itech hualmopachozque in tlaneltoquiliztli, inic quitelchiuhque, inic quiìyaque in tlateotoquiliztli, inic omotlapololtìtinemico in tlalticpac, in tlayohuayan in
mixtecomac ic oquinnemiti in tlacatecolotl; ihuan inic çẽca i-
techtzinco motzatzilizq̃, tlaquauhtlamatizque;[3] oquimonequilti inic nican omentin tlaca[4] oquinmottititzino in yancuican yhuan
oinmàçehualtic in itlaçòixiptlatzin izçenquizcaichpochtzintli toçihuapillàtocatzin in nican inahuac altepetl Mexìco moyetztica in
quimottititzino in Iuan Diego in oncan Tepeyacac Guadalupe:
niman yè in ixiptlatzin moteneuhtzinoa Remedios quimottititzino
in Dõ Iuan in oncan Totoltepec,

in quimottilitzino in icpac Tepetzintli metitlã moyetzinòticatca,[5] in
axcan oncan ìcac iTeocaltzin; Quimohuiquili in ichan oncan achi
quezqui xihuitl quimopiali, auh çatepan quimochìchihuilili çe
teocaltzintli in ixpan in ical inic ompa conmìquanili. Auh in ye
achi quexquich cahuitl in ompa moyetztica; itech motlali huey
cocoliztli in Dõ Iuan auh in omottac, in ca ye tlanahui in aoc huel
maquiçaz moquetzaz, quintlatlauhti in ipilhuan maçehualtzitzintin
totoltepec tlaca inic quihuicazque Tepeyacac in ompa moyetztica
izçenquizcaichpochtli Totlaçònantzin Guadalupe in àço quipa-
nahuia ome leguas inic quihuècaitztica in oncan totoltepec. Yèica
quimatia in quenin quimopàtili in ilhuicac Çihuapilli in Iuan
Bernardino Quauhtitlã chane iTlàtzin in Iuan Diego izça ye no yè
itech catca huei cocoliztli; ihuan in ye ixquich tlamahuiçolli ye
quimochihuilia. Niman ic tlapechco contecaque quihuicaque in
ompa Tepeyacac: auh in ocontecato in ixpantzinco ilhuicac

---

[1]*Itepantlàtoltzin*: probably for *itepantlàtoliztzin*, parallel to the following
noun and the usual word in any event.

[2]*In imoztlayoc*: this phrase may go with what precedes. The translation
would be: "the epidemic began to subside the next day. No longer were
many people buried, . . ."

[3]*Tlaquauhtlamatizque*: the meaning is given by Molina under "Tetech

precious, revered mother, the epidemic would begin to subside. The next day,[2] not many people were being buried any longer, and finally perhaps two or three people as the epidemic came to an end.

IN THE BEGINNING, when the Christian faith had just arrived here in the land that today is called New Spain, in many ways the heavenly Lady, the consummate Virgin Saint Mary, cherished, aided, and defended the local people so that they might entirely give themselves and adhere to the faith. As a result they despised and abhorred the idolatry in which they had been wandering about in confusion on the earth, in the night and darkness in which the demon had made them live. In order that they might invoke her fervently and trust in her fully,[3] she saw fit to reveal herself for the first time to two people here.[4] They attained the precious images of the consummate Virgin, our Queen, which are here near the altepetl of Mexico; she appeared to Juan Diego at Tepeyacac Guadalupe, and she revealed the image that is called Remedios to don Juan at Totoltepec.

She revealed herself to him [don Juan] on top of a hill, among maguey plants, where her temple stands today. He took her to his home and kept her there for several years, and afterwards he outfitted a small temple for her in front of his house and moved her there. And when she had been there for some time, don Juan contracted a serious illness. When it was seen that he was fatally ill, that he would no longer be able to escape or to get up, he asked his children, the humble Totoltepec commoners, to take him to Tepeyacac where the consummate Virgin, our precious mother of Guadalupe, is, which is perhaps more than two leagues distant from Totoltepec, because he knew how the heavenly Lady had healed Juan Bernardino, resident of Quauhtitlan and uncle of Juan Diego, upon whom a very great illness had likewise come, and had worked all the [other] miracles. Thereupon they laid him on a litter, took him to

---

nitlaꝗtlamati" (VM, Nahuatl/Span., f. 106).

   [4]*Nican omentin tlaca*. The phrase is very close indeed to *nican tlaca*, "local (indigenous) people." Probably that is the intention. Yet in that case the wording should have been *omentin nican tlaca*.

   [5]*Moyetzinòticatca*: another case of *tz* for *tztz* (see at n. 7, pp. 62–63, and n. 1, p. 88).

Çihuapilli Totlaçònantzin de Guadalupe, niman ye ic quimocho-
quiztlatlauhtilia ixpantzinco mocnoteca, mocnomati, quimìtlani-
lilia inic ma quimocnelili, ma quimopàtili in itlallo, in içoquio,
àço huel oc çemilhuitzintli quimonemitiliz in itlalticpactzinco, inic
huel quimotlayecoltiliz in yèhuatzin, ihuã in itlaçòconetzin; auh
quimopaccaçelili in icnohuàcatzintli in itlatlatlauhtiliz, çenca mo-
pàpaquiltia, mohuehuetzquitia in oquimottili, quimotlatlaçòtilia,
inic quimononochilia, ximoquetza ca ye otipàtic, ximocuepa in
ompa in mochan: auh nimitznahuatia in icpac tepetl in canin ìcac
î[1] metl in oncan tiquittac nixiptla xicquetza çe Teòcaltzintli in oncan yez; ihuan oc cequi ic quimonànahuatili in tlein quichihuaz:
auh niman ìquac pàtic. Auh in o yuh conmotlatlauhtili izçenca
quitlaçòcamati, in iteicneliltzin, hualmocuep in ichan ça icxipan,
aocmo quinapalòque. Auh in oàçico nimã quineltili, quiquetz in
iTeòcaltzin in itlaçòixiptlatzin in ilhuicac Çihuapilli moteneuhtzinoa Remedios in oncan axcan moyetztica. Auh in o yuh yecauh in iTeocaltzin huel yèhuatzin in omocalaquitzinoto, inòma-
tzinco omoquetzinoto,[2] in ipan altartzin in yuh axcan moyetztica,
yhuan in yuh ìcuiliuhtica in ipan in ixquich itlamahuiçoltzin.

NIcan ipan altepetl Mexìco çemè caxtiltecapipiltin itoca Don
Antonio Carauajal quihuicac oc ce telpocatzin[3] ihuanyolqui ompa
ya in Tollantzinco, auh inic onquizquè in oncan Tepeyacac, oc
oncan calàq̃[4] in iteopanchantzinco izçenquizcaichpochtli Totlaçònantzin Guadalupe, oc oncã moteochiuhtiquizque quimotlàpal-
huìtiquizque in ilhuicac TlatòcaÇihuapilli inic quinmopalehuiliz,
quimomanahuiliz;[5] ihuan qualli quinmàxitiliz in ompa ic hui.
Auh in ohualquizque, in ye nènemi òtlica ic mononotztàque in
itechpatzinco izcenquizcaichpochtli in yuh monexiti in itlaçòixiptlayotzin, in huel huey tlamahuiçoltica: ihuan in ye ixquich
nepapan tlamahuiçolli ye quimochihuilia, inic quinmocnelilia in
aquìque itechtzinco motzatzilia;

auh in ye òtlatocatihui in iCaballo in ipan yetihuia Telpocatzin,

---

[1]î: for *in*, *im*, or *î*. It may be that the printer lacked the capacity to put a
tilde over an *i*.

[2]*Omoquetzinoto*: another example of *tz* for *tztz*, with the same roots as
in two other cases.

[3]*Telpocatzin*: *telpocatl*, already a rather pejorative version of *telpochtli*,

Tepeyacac, and went to lay him down before the heavenly Lady, our precious mother of Guadalupe. Then he prayed to her tearfully, he bowed down and humbled himself before her, and asked her to do him the favor of healing his earthly body. Perhaps she would cause him to live for another brief day on her earth, so that he could serve her and her precious child. The compassionate one received his prayers benevolently. She was very happy, she smiled when she saw him, and she showed him affection, as she told him, "Get up! you have already been cured. Return to your home. And I command you that on top of the hill, where the maguey plants stand, where you saw my image, you build a small temple, where it will be." And she commanded him to do various other things. At that very moment he recovered. And when he had addressed her with many thanks for her benevolence, he returned home on foot. They no longer carried him in their arms. When he arrived, he immediately carried it out; he built the small temple for the precious image of the heavenly Lady, called Remedios, where she is now. After her temple was finished, she herself entered, all by herself she went to stand on the altar as she is today and as she is depicted in all her miracles.

HERE IN THE altepetl of Mexico one of the Spanish noblemen, named don Antonio Carvajal, took a young fellow,[2] a relative of his, with him when he went to Tulancingo. When they passed through Tepeyacac, they first went into the churchly home of the consummate Virgin, our precious mother of Guadalupe; they stopped a while to pray there, they stopped by to greet the heavenly Queen so that she might aid and defend them and cause them to arrive safely where they were going. When they had come back out and were traveling along, on the way they went along talking with one another about the consummate Virgin, how she revealed her precious image by a very great miracle, and how she had worked all the different kinds of miracles, by which she did good to those who invoked her.

As the horse on which the young fellow was riding was go-

"youth," is here further downgraded by the omission of the absolute singular ending.

[4]*Calàq̃.* standard *calacq̃* (= *calacque*). See pp. 80–81, n. 4.

[5]*Quimomanahuiliz*: for *quinmomanahuiliz*.

çan ipan hualhuetz[1] inic[2] tlahuelcuic, cuix noçè itla quimauhtì, huel ihui in onehuac, motlaloa, atlauhtla, tepexic, texcalla, in oc nen ixquich itlàpal ic quitititzaya freno aoc huel quixîco,[3] àço media legua in quitocti, in oc nen quitzacuilizquia in intehuicalhuan,[4] niman aoc huel mochiuhque yuhqui, in ècatoco ic yauh, niman quipoloto, in momatque àmo[5] ye cana oquitetextilito, canoço huel ohuìcã in canin otlamelauhtiquiz, ca huel atlauhtla, texcalla;

auh quimonequilti in Totecuiyo, ihuan izçenquizcaicnohuàcatzintli itlaçòmahuizNantzin quimomaquixtili in ìquac quipãtilito, in ipan àçito ca moquetztìcac in Caballo tolotìcac, iuhqui oquicòcolo in ima, niman aoc huel molinia, auh in telpocatzin çe icxi ic pilcac estribotitech otlatzicò. Auh in oquittaque çenca huel oquimahuiçòq̃ inyoltica, ihuã in nimã àquen in mochiuh, manoçe cana omococò, nimã ic quinapalòque, quihualquixtìque in icxi: auh in omoquetz quitlàtlanìque quenin omaquiz in àtle ipan omochiuh, auh in yèhuatl quimilhui

ca ye oanquimottilìque in quenin ìquac otihualquizq̃ Mexìco oncan tihualquiztiquizq̃ ichantzinco in ilhuicac Çihuapilli totlaçòNantzin Guadalupe oncan tichualmahuiçòtehuaque in itlaçòixiptlatzin tictotlatlauhtilique, auh çatepan òtlica ictohualnonotztiàque[6] in ixquich tlamahuiçolli ye quimochihuilia, in quenin huel huey tlamahuiçoltica monexiti in itlaçòixiptlatzin; auh ca huel çêca çenmochi ipan ya in notlalnamiquiliz huel nicnoyolloti.[7] Auh yè in ìquac o yuh ninottac, in huel oninoohuìcanaquì in aoccã huel nimaquiçaz ca yeppa nimiquiz, nipòpolihuiz, in niman aoctle oncatca nopalehuiloca, çã nimã ìquac çenmoch îca in noyollo nicnotza-

---

[1]*Çan ipan hualhuetz*: *çan ipan* can mean "somehow" (VM, Nahuatl/ Span., f. 14v). Another possible interpretation is "he [the boy] fell off it [the horse]." But in that event the horse would have been dragging him along on the ground during its whole wild charge, and later he is said to have been pulling on the reins. Yet in Stradanus he seems to be being dragged.

[2]*Inic*: the direction of the causality is not entirely clear. Conceivably the horse fell because of its wildness or fright.

[3]*Quixîco*: the verb *xicoa*, best known in other senses, can mean "to best,

ing along the road, somehow it fell down;[1] as a result[2] it went wild, or perhaps something frightened it. It took off with great impetus and ran through ravines, past precipices and crags, while he tried with all his strength to pull on the reins. He was unable to control it;[3] it ran him for perhaps half a league. His companions[4] tried to intercept it, but they could by no means do so; it went as if carried by the wind. Then they lost sight of it, and thought that it might[5] have pulverized him somewhere. Indeed it was a very dangerous place that it was heading straight toward, a place of many ravines and crags.

But our Lord and the perfectly compassionate one, his precious, honored mother, saw fit to free him. When they found him, what they came upon was that the horse had stopped, it had bowed its head, and its legs were as though bent. It was entirely unable to move, and the young fellow was stuck in a stirrup, hanging by one foot. When they saw him, they greatly marveled in their hearts; there was nothing at all wrong with him, nor was he hurt anywhere. Thereupon they took him in their arms and released his foot. When he got up, they asked him how he had escaped without anything happening to him, and he said to them,

> You saw how when we left Mexico, we passed by the home of the heavenly Lady, our precious mother of Guadalupe. Before leaving we marveled at her precious image and prayed to her, and afterwards on the road we went along talking to one another about all the miracles that she has worked and how her precious image appeared by a very great miracle. Absolutely everything found its way into my memory, I took it very much to heart.[7] So when I saw that I was put in great danger, that there was no way I could escape, that I would soon die and perish, that there was no longer any help for me whatever, just at that very moment

---

to get control of"; see Lockhart 1992, p. 400 (line 4 of the first stanza of Nahuatl), and p. 588, n. 13.

[4]*Intehuicalhuan*: since the possessor is singular, the form should be *itehuicalhuan*. The usual word for "companion" is *-tlahuical* (VM, Span./ Nahuatl, f. 28), not *-tehuical*.

[5]*Àmo*: probably for *àço*, "perhaps."

[6]*Ictohualnonotztiàque*: for *tictohualnonotztiàque*.

[7]*Nicnoyolloti*: see above, pp. 54–55, n. 3.

tzilili izçenquizcaichpochtzintli ilhuicac Çihuapilli Totlaçònantzin Guadalupe inic ma nechmocnoittili, ma nechmo-
palehuili; auh ca çan nimã ìquac onicnottili in quenin huel
yèhuatzin in iuh monexitìtica in ipan itlaçòixiptlayotzin in
toÇihuapillatocatzin Guadalupe in onechmopalehuili, in o-
nechmomaquixtili, oquimotzitzquilili in ifreno in Caballo,
inic nimã omoquetz, oquimotlacamachiti, iuhqui in ixpantzinco omopachò, omotlanquacolo in yuhqui quenin o ipã
anmaxitico:
huel çenca ic quimoyectenehuilìque in ilhuicac Çihuapilli niman
ic òtlatocaque.
CEppa çe Caxtiltecatl ixpantzinco motlanquaquetztìcaya in ilhuicac Çihuapilli totlaçòNantzin Guadalupe quimotlatlauhtilìticatca.
Auh mochiuh coton in mecatl ic pilcaya çe huey lampara in huel
yetic in ixpãtzinco pilcaya; auh niman iquapan huallamelauh,
huel ipan in itzontecon huetzico, auh in ixquichtin oncan ocatca
omomatque àço niman omic àco[1] oquiquaxaman, auh ànoçe huel
oquicocò; yèica ca huel huècapan in hualehuac: Auh àmo çaniyo
in àquen mochiuh, in àcan mococò yece in lampara niman àcan
pachiuh, noçe tepiton ìtlacauh ihuan in tehuilotl àmo tlapan, auh
in azeite oncan ocatca àmo onoquiuh ihuan àmo oçeuh inic tlatla-
ticatca, huel çêca quimahuiçòq̃ mochi tlacatl in ixquich tlamahuiçolli çã çemi[2] quimochihuili in ilhuicac Çihuapilli.

IN yèhuatl Licenciado Iuan Vazquez de Acuña Vicario catca in
huel miac xihuitl oncan motlàpiali. Çeppa mochiuh ye quimochi-
huiliz Missa in oncan Altar mayor auh o moch çèçeuh in candela;
auh in Sachristan oc ya in quitlatito, yè inic çenca yèyecani[3] in
oncan, auh in Teopixqui mochialìticatca inic tlatlaz candelas,
quittac in itech itonameyotzin ilhuicac Çihuapilli hualquiz ome
yuhqui in tlemiahuatl, noçe iuhqui, in tlapetlanillotl quitlàtlatico
in candelas necoccampa: huel çenca quimahuiçòque inin tlama-

---

[1] *Àco*: for *àço*.

[2] *Çã çemi*. This phrase is well known in the meanings "finally, for this
last time," etc. (VM, Nahuatl/Span., f. 13v, under "ça cemi"). *Cemi* by
itself is recorded in the modern Nahuatl of Tetelcingo with the gloss
"always" (Brewer and Brewer 1971, p. 221; also referred to in DK, p. 29).
We are convinced, however, that the true key to the passage is in the Miguel

with all my heart I called on the consummate Virgin, the heavenly Lady, our precious mother of Guadalupe, to have pity on me and help me. Just at that very moment I saw her, just as she herself appears in the precious image of our Queen of Guadalupe. She helped and rescued me; she grabbed the horse's reins, so that it stopped immediately and obeyed her. Like one bowing before her, it knelt down as it was when you found it.

They praised the heavenly Lady very greatly, and thereupon they traveled on.

ONCE A SPANIARD was kneeling before the heavenly Lady, our precious mother of Guadalupe, praying to her. It happened that the rope broke from which a large lamp was hanging; it was very heavy, and it was hanging in front of her. Right away it went straight toward his head, it fell right on his skull. All those who were there believed that he had died immediately or that it had smashed his head, or that perhaps it had seriously injured him, for it fell from a great height. But not only was he not harmed and suffered no injury of any sort, but the lamp was not crushed anywhere at all, nor was it damaged in the slightest. The glass did not break, the oil that was in it did not spill, and the flame that was burning did not go out. Everyone was very greatly astonished at all the miracles that the heavenly Lady worked at a single time.[2]

LICENCIATE JUAN Vásquez de Acuña, former vicar, was in charge there for very many years. Once it happened that he was about to say mass at the main altar and all the candles went out. The sacristan meanwhile went away to light [others], because it was very windy[3] there, and the priest was waiting for the candles to be burning. He saw two things like tassels of flame or lightning come out of the rays of the heavenly Lady and come to light the candles on both sides. This miracle very much aston-

---

Sánchez version of this episode (IVM, p. 175), which says that it caused astonishment in all those present, "viendo en vn milagro tantos milagros."

[3]*Yèyecani*: The word *eecatl* (*èecatl*), "wind," has a frequent variant *yeyecatl*. The related verb *eeca* "for the wind to blow" is not much seen in texts, but it exists (VM, Nahuatl/Span., f. 28). The present form is a *-ni* agentive of that verb, used in a typically adjectival fashion.

huiçolli in ixquichtin oncan iteopanchantzinco catcaya.[1]
IN ìquac huel yancuican ilhuicac Çihuapilli quimottititzino in
Iuan Diego ihuan in huei tlamahuiçoltica monexiti in itlaçòixiptlatzin, huel çenca miec in tlamahuiçolli quimochihuilì; yuh mittoa
no ihuã ìquac motlapò in ameyaltzintli, in itepotzca[2] iteòcaltzin
ilhuicac Çihuapilli tonatiuh iquiçayampa, huel oncã in canin qui-
monamiquilito in Iuã Diego in ìquac quitlayahualhui tepetzintli
inic àmo quimottilizquia ilhuicac Çihuapilli in oc acattopa quinec
quinotzaz Teopixqui, in quiyolcuitizquia, in quiçencahuazquia in
iTlatzin Iuan Bernardino in huel tlanauhtoya, huel oncan in qui-
moyacatzacuilili, ihuan in oncan conmihuali xochitequito in icpac
tepetzintli, no ihuan oncan conmottitili in tlalmantzintli in oncan
moquetzaz teòcaltzintli, ihuan in oncan ca ic çen quihualmihuali
inic quittaz Tlàtohuani Obispo in quimotitlanilili xochitl in ineltica, ihuan in inezca, itlanequiliztzin, ic mochihuaz iteòcaltzin; in
ye o moch hualmittotiquiz. Inin atzintli in oncan meya, maçihui
in màcoquetza ic moloni, ic momoloca àmo ic pepeyahua, ma-
noçè huey quitoca[3] ca çan huel tepitzin, ihuan huel chipactic
àhuiac, yece àmo huelic achi yuhqui in xoxococ, quimopàchihuia in ixquich cocoliztli nepapan, in aquìque izçenyollò-
cacopa conì, noçe ic màaltia; ic ipampa àmo çan tlapohualli
tlamahuiçolli ye quimochihuilia izçenquizcaichpochtzintli ilhuicac
Çihuapilli Totlaçònantzin Santa M A R I A de Guadalupe.

CE Caxtillan çihuatl chane catca in nican ipan altepetl Mexìco çan
ixpeuh[4] in ye poçauhtiuh in ìte yuhqui in ìtexihui, iuhqui in ye
cuitlaxitiniz: otlayèyecòque in titici Caxtilteca, nepapan pàtli ic
quipàtiaya; niman àtle quinamic,[5] manoçe quimopàchihui, ilhuice
ohueixtitia, ye màtlactli metztli in itech ca in icocoliz, yhuan ye
huel yuh ca in iyollo ca niman aoc huel pàtiz, ca ic miquiz intlacamo yèhuatzin quimopàtiliz in ilhuicac Çihuapilli, çenquizcaichpochtli Santa MARIA de Guadalupe: auh tlanahuati inic quitla-
pechhuizque ompa quihuicazque in tepeyacac in ichantzinco
ilhuicac Çihuapilli: Auh yohuatzinco conehuiltìque; auh in o-

---

[1]*Catcaya*: an inelegant variant of *catca*, not often seen in ecclesiastical
texts.
[2]*Itepotzca*: apparently for *itepotzco*. Possibly the intention was *itepotzco
ca* (*cà*).
[3]*Quitoca*: the verb *toca* often has to do with forcefully running water
carrying things away. Here, however, it is unclear just what the subject and

ished all those who were there in her churchly home.

WHEN FOR THE very first time the heavenly Lady showed herself to Juan Diego and her precious image very miraculously appeared, she worked very many miracles. It is said that also at that time the spring opened up which is behind the temple of the heavenly Lady to the east, in the very place where she went to meet Juan Diego when he had gone around the hill so that the heavenly Lady might not see him, since he first wanted to call a friar to hear the confession of and prepare his uncle, Juan Bernardino, who lay very gravely ill. It was right there that she intercepted him and sent him to go cut flowers on the top of the hill. It was also where she showed him the level ground where the temple was to be built, and where she sent him for the last time to see the lord bishop, to whom she sent flowers as a proof and sign of her wish that her temple was to be built. All of this was said earlier in passing. Where this water gushes out, although it flies up as it gushes and bubbles, it still does not overflow, nor does it [fly out?][3] greatly, only a very little. It is very clean and fragrant, but not good tasting, somewhat as if acidic. It is effective with all different kinds of illnesses for those who in good faith drink it or bathe in it. For that reason the miracles that the consummate Virgin, the heavenly Lady, our precious mother Saint Mary of Guadalupe, has worked are innumerable.

THE STOMACH of a Spanish woman, who was a resident here in the altepetl of Mexico, began for no reason[4] to swell as if it were hydropic, as if it would burst. The Spanish physicians tried different kinds of medicine by which to cure her; absolutely nothing helped[5] or worked, but it kept on growing all the more. It was now ten months that she had the illness, and she was quite certain that she could never get well again, that she would die of it, unless the heavenly Lady, the consummate Virgin, Saint Mary of Guadalupe, would heal her. She directed them to carry her on a litter and take her to Tepeyacac to the home of the

---

object might be. Probably the verb has some specialized sense unknown to us.

   [4]*Ixpeuh. Ixpehua* is glossed "to begin arguments without reason" (VM, Nahuatl/Span., f. 46v); presumably it can mean for anything to begin without reason.

   [5]*quinamic*: literally, "fit it."

conàxitito in iteopanchantzinco, ixpantzinco contecato, nimã ye
ic conmotlatlauhtilia moch ica in iyollo inic ma quimocnoyttili,
ma quimopàtili; ixpantzinco choca, mocnopechteca: auh quìtlan
ma tepitzin macò[1] in iamealtzin inic coniz, auh in o yuh conîc
nimã ic yamanix, peuh in ye cochi, auh in ye oquipanahui
nepantla tonatiuh, in ye tziliniz çe, in quihuicaque, oc hualquiz-
que quiahuac tlatlamahuiçoto, ça içel quihualcauhtiquizque in
oquic oncochi: Onyamanix: auh ceme in maçehualtzitzintin in
oncan nètollèque tlàtlachpantinemi Teopan, in ye oquittac itzintlã
hualquiça huel temàmauhtì cohuatl, çenmatl, ihuã çemiztetl[2] inic
hueyac ihuan huel tomahuac, huel çenca omomauhtì niman qui-
tzàtzili in Caxtillan çihuatl cocoxcatzintli, niman ic içatehuac,
meuhtehuac, huel çenca mìçahui momauhtì, tzatzàtzic inic
tenotza, nimã oncan cõmictìq̃ in cohuatl; auh nimã ìquac pàtic,
opachiuh in ìte, auh oc onahuilhuiti in oncan, inic çeçemilhuitl
quimotlatlauhtiliaya in ilhuicac Çihuapilli in oquimocnelili in o-
quimopàtili; auh in ìquac hualmocuep aocmo quihualnapalòq̃ ça
huallacxipàhui[3] ye huel pactihuitz aoctle mà quicocoa.

CE Caxtiltecapilli chane in nican ipan altepetl Mexìco huel chicahuac inic quicocoaya in itzontecon, ihuan in inacaz, yuhqui ye
cuitlaxitiniz, niman àtle quimopàchihui, aoc huel quìyohuiaya:
tlanahuati inic huicoz in ompa itlaçòchantzinco izçenquizcaichpochtzintli Totlaçònantzin Guadalupe. Auh in oàçito ixpantzinco,
huel izceyollòcacopa[4] quimotlatlauhtilì inic ma quimopalehuilì,[5]
ma quimopàtili; auh omonètolti, ca intla oquimopàtili ixpantzinco
quihuenchihuaz ce tzontecomatl iztac teocuitlatl, auh çan niman
ìquac in oàçito opàtic. Auh in yuh chiucnahuilhuiti in ichantzinco
ilhuicac Çihuapilli hualmocuep in ichan hualpactia, niman aoctle
quicocoa.

---

[1]*Macò*: the *o* is not followed by glottal stop; it is inherently long, but
not so pronounced in final position.
[2]*Çemiztetl*: *iztetl* and *iztitl* are variants. See n. 3, pp. 88–89. The *matl*,
here translated as "fathom," could be seven to ten feet when used as a mea-
sure for agricultural land. In measuring houses and house plots around

heavenly Lady. Very early in the morning they started her on her way, and when they got her to her churchly home, they laid her down before her. Thereupon she prayed to her with all her heart that she would have pity on her and cure her. She wept before her, prostrated herself, and asked to be given a little bit of her spring water to drink. After she drank it, her body temperature moderated, and she fell asleep. When it was past midday and the bell was about to strike one, those who had brought her came back outside the building for a while to go look around. They came out leaving her all alone while she slept and her temperature moderated, and one of the humble commoners who had taken a vow there to sweep at the church saw a very frightening snake come out from under her, a fathom and one span[2] in length, and very thick. He was very frightened and immediately cried out to the Spanish woman who was sick. At that she awoke and got up. She was very much startled and frightened and repeatedly cried out to summon someone. Then they killed the snake there; at that very moment she got well and her stomach went down. She spent four more days there, in order to pray daily to the heavenly Lady who had done her this favor and healed her. When she came back, they no longer carried her in their arms; she came back just on foot. Now she came greatly rejoicing; nothing was ailing her any more.

THE HEAD AND ears of a Spanish nobleman, a resident here in the altepetl of Mexico, pained him very badly, as if they would burst; absolutely nothing helped him. He could endure it no longer, and he directed that he be taken to the precious home of the consummate Virgin, our precious mother of Guadalupe. When he arrived in her presence, he prayed to her with all his heart to help him and cure him. He vowed that when she had cured him, he would make an offering to her of a head of silver. Just at the very moment he got there, he was cured. After he had spent nine days at the home of the heavenly Lady, he returned home rejoicing. Absolutely nothing more was ailing him.

Mexico City, it was apparently closer to two Spanish yards, the approximate quantity we imagine as intended here.

[3]*Huallacxipàhui*: for *huallacxipāhui*.

[4]*Izceyollòcacopa*: standard *icenyollòcacopa*.

[5]*Quimopalehuilì*: the final *i* is neither long nor followed by glottal stop.

CE çihuatzintli itoca Cathalina ìtexihuia, auh in oquittac in nimã aoctle quimopàchihuia, in ye huellanauhtoc, auh in titiçi quìttoa aocmo mehuaz ca yeppa miquiz: tlatlatlauhti inic quihuicazque in ompa iteopanchantzinco in ilhuicac Çihuapilli Totlaçònantzin Guadalupe: auh in o yuh càxitito huel moch ica in iyollo quimotlatlauhtili inic ma quimopàtili, niman ic quihualquixtìtiàque ome tlacatl quihualtzìtzitzquìtiàque, huel ixquich itlàpal quichiuh inic àçito in oncan ca îameyaltzin; auh huel moch ica in iyollo inic conîc in atl oncan meya, nimã ic oncan opàtic, iuhquin èecatl nohuiampa itech hualquiz, ilhuice îcamacpa inic conîc in atl. Auh in oncalac iteopanchantzinco Çihuapilli ye opàtic aoctle quicocoa.

CE San Francisco Teopixcatzintli in àtle icactzin itocatzin Fray Pedro de Valderrama huel tlanahuia in quicocoa, çe ixopil in huel otlanauh in niman huel aoc pàtiz intlacamo quicotonilizque, yèica itech omotlali in huey qualocatl niman ic ìçiuhca quihuicati-huetzque in ompa itlaçòchantzinco in ilhuicac Çihuapilli Guada-lupe auh in o yuh ixpantzinco àçito niman ic quitòton in tzotzo-màtli, ic quimiliuhticatca[1] ixopil, quimottitili in ilhuicac Çihua-pilli: ihuan huel moch ica in iyollo quimotlatlauhtili inic ma quimopàtili; auh ca çan niman ìquac opàtic, auh in ye pactica ça icxipan omocuep in ompa Pachòcan.

OC no çe Caxtiltecalpìlli[2] itoca Don Luys de Castilla çe icxi huel poçahuac, auh in ye huel otlanauh, ye cocoyoca[3] inic palani in niman aoctle quimopàchihuia inic quipàtia in titici. Auh ye huel yuh ca in iyollo ca ic miquiz, yuh mìttoa quimolhuili in tlacpac Teopixqui omoteneuh, in quenin yèhuatl quimopàtili in ilhuicac Çihuapilli Totlaçònantzin Guadalupe niman ic tlanahuati quichi-huazque in teocuitlapitzq̃ çe iztac teocuitlaicxitl in ixquich huey in icxi; niman ic quihualmotitlanilili; inic oncan iteopanchan-tzinco ixpantzinco quipilozque huel icenyollòcacopa imactzin-co hualmocauh inic quimopàtiliz. Auh in titlàtli quicahuaco in ìquac ompa hualquiz, ye momiquiliznequi, ye huellanauhtoc, auh in ìquac mocuep in ipan àçito, ye pactica, ye oquimopàtili in

---

[1]*Quimiliuhticatca: quimiloa,* "to wrap something," implies the existence of intransitive *quimilihui,* "to be wrapped."

[2]*Caxtiltecalpìlli:* for *Caxtiltecapilli*; the *i* bearing the grave accent is

A HUMBLE woman named Catalina had hydropsy. When she saw that nothing whatever did her any good, that she lay fatally ill, and the physicians said that she would never rise again and would soon die, she begged them to take her to the churchly home of the heavenly Lady, our precious mother of Guadalupe. When they had brought her there, she prayed to her with all her heart that she might cure her. Thereupon two persons brought her back outside, holding her as they came. She used every ounce of her strength to get to where her spring is. With all her heart she drank the water where it gushed forth. Thereupon she was healed there; like the wind [the swelling] came out of her everywhere, especially from her mouth, as she drank the water. By the time she went into the Lady's churchly home, she was already cured; nothing more ailed her.

A DISCALCED Franciscan friar named fray Pedro de Valderrama was gravely ill; one of his toes pained him. He was in great extremity; he could no longer recover at all unless they should cut the toe off, because a large cancer had grown on it. Thereupon they hurriedly took him to the precious home of the heavenly Lady of Guadalupe. When he arrived in her presence, he undid the cloth in which his toe was wrapped.[1] He showed it to the heavenly Lady, and with all his heart he prayed to her to heal him. Just at that very moment he was healed, and rejoicing he returned on foot to Pachuca.

FURTHER, a Spanish nobleman named don Luis de Castilla had a very swollen foot, and he was very gravely ill; [the foot] was full of holes[3] from decay, and absolutely nothing with which the physicians were treating him was helping. He was very sure that he would die from it. It is said that the abovementioned friar told him how the heavenly Lady, our precious mother of Guadalupe, cured him. Thereupon he directed the goldsmiths to make a silver foot, the same size as his own. Thereupon he sent it to be hung in her churchly home, in her presence. With all his heart he left himself in her hands so that she might cure him. When the messenger left to come to deliver it, he [don Luis] was about to die, he already lay in extremity. But when [the messenger]

---

neither long nor followed by glottal stop.

    [3]*Cocoyoca*: a frequentative of *coyoni* "to get holes" (DK, p. 43).

ilhuicac Çihuapilli.

CE Sachristan itoca Iuan Pabon in oncan motlacuitlahuiaya in
iteopanchantzinco ilhuicac Çihuapilli totlaçònantzin Guadalupe
quipiaya çe piltzintli[1] auh itech motlali in quechpoçahualiztli, ye
huel otlanauh, ye momiquiliznequi, aoc huel cana in iiyo; Quihuicac ixpantzinco, auh ic conmamatelò in azeite ilamparatzin ic
tlatla; auh çan nimā ìquac pàtic quimocnelili in ilhuicac Çihuapilli.

YN oc itzinècan, in oc ipeuhyan in ìquac monexîti in itlaçòixiptlatzin izçenquizcaichpochtzintli Totlaçònantzin Guadalupe in
nican tlaca tlàtoque Pipiltin huel ìtechtzinco[2] motzatziliaya inic
quinmopalehuiliaya, inic quinmomanahuiliaya in innetolinniliz-
pan, ihuan in inmiquiztempan, içenmactzinco mocahuaya çemè
yèhuan in,[3] in tlàtohuani catca Dõ Francisco Quetzlalmamalitzin[4]
Teotihuàcan in ìquac xixin in altepetl in huel cactimoman, in
niman aocac mocauhtiquiz inic àmo quinmocahualiztlama-
chiltiaya in San Francisco Teopixque, in quinequia Tlàtohuani
Visorrey Don Luys de Velasco yèhuantzitzin in San Augustin
Teopixque quinmocuitlahuìtzinozque, huel ic cenca netolinniliztli
quittaque in altepehuàque. Auh in intlàtocauh Don Francisco,
ihuan in ipiloan[5] ça motlàtlatitinemia, yèica huel nohuian temoloya; auh oncan hualla izça tlaçaccan[6] in Azcapotzalco, auh
ichtaca quihualmotlatlauhtiliaya in ilhuicac Çihuapilli Guadalupe
ma quimoyollotili in itlaçòconetzin in Visorrey, ihuan in tlatòque
Audiencia Real inic tlapòpolhuililozq̃ altepehuàque inic huel
mocuepazque in inchan, ihuan oc çeppa macozquè in San Francisco Teopixque, auh huel yuh mochiuh, ca otlapòpolhuililoque
in altepehuàque, ihuan in intlatòcauh in inpillohuan, ihuan oc
çeppa macoque in San Francisco Teopixque, inic quinmocuitlahuizque, ihuan mochintin hualmocuepque in inchan aocmo mà
ic toliniloque: mochiuh ye ipan xihuitl mil y quinientos y
cincuenta y ocho, no ihuan in ye imiquiztempan in Dõ Francisco
huel içenmactzinco mocauh in ilhuicac Çihuapilli Totlaçònantzin

---

[1]*Piltzintli.* A boy may have been in the mind of the writer, as in the
Stradanus engraving, but the Nahuatl here does not specify gender, and we
have kept the translation neutral even though "it" is no longer very idiomatic English in speaking of children.

[2]*Ìtechtzinco:* the *i* marked with a grave accent is long and not followed
by glottal stop.

returned, he found [don Luis] healthy; the heavenly Lady had cured him.

A SACRISTAN named Juan Pavón, who took care of the churchly home of the heavenly Lady, our precious mother of Guadalupe, had a small child,[1] and it contracted a swelling of the neck. It was gravely ill and about to die; it was no longer able to breathe. He took it before her and anointed it with the oil that burns in her lamp. At that very moment it was healed, favored by the heavenly Lady.

IN THE BEGINNINGS, when the precious image of the consummate Virgin, our precious mother of Guadalupe, appeared, the local people who were rulers and nobles called upon her very much to aid and defend them in their afflictions, and at the point of death they would leave themselves entirely in her hands. One of these was the ruler don Francisco Quetzalmamalitzin of Teotihuacan. At that time the altepetl dispersed and was entirely deserted, with not a person left, because they opposed giving up the friars of Saint Francis, for the lord Viceroy don Luis de Velasco wanted the friars of Saint Augustine to take care of them, which the citizens of the altepetl saw as a great deprivation. Their ruler, don Francisco, and his nobles went about hiding in various places, because they were being sought everywhere. The last place he came to was Azcapotzalco. He was secretly praying to the heavenly Lady of Guadalupe that her precious child might inspire the viceroy and the lords of the Royal Audiencia so that the citizens of the altepetl would be forgiven, be able to return to their homes, and be given the friars of Saint Francis again. And that is exactly what happened. The citizens of the altepetl and their ruler and their nobles were pardoned, and they were given the friars of Saint Francis to take care of them again. They all came back to their homes, they were no longer bothered over this matter in any way. It happened in the year 1558. And also when he was at the point of death, don Francisco placed himself entirely in the hands of the heavenly

<hr>

[3]*Yèhuan in*. This odd formation, with *in* left hanging, is apparently to be explained by a missing (or possibly too low) *t* between the two words. The intention would have been *yèhuantin*.

[4]*Quetzlalmamalitzin*: for *Quetzalmamalitzin*.

[5]*Ipiloan*: for *ipillohuan*, as below.

[6]*Tlaçaccan*: for standard *tlatzaccan*.

Guadalupe inic ipan motlàtoltiz in iyolia, in ianima, auh mohuenchiuhta in ixpantzinco, in iuh neztica in ipā itestamento in
huel tlayacatitica itlàtol, itlatecpan, mochiuh ic omilhuitl mani
Março in ipan xihuitl mil y quinientos y sesenta y tres.

IN ye yuh moyetztica in itlaçòchantzinco, izçenquizcaichpochtzintli ilhuicac Çihuapilli Guadalupe àmo çan quexquich, àmo
çan tlapohualli in tlamahuiçolli quimochihuili, inic quinmocneli-
liaya in nican tlaca ihuan in Caxtilteca, ça çe in ixquichtin nepapan tlaca itechtzinco motzàtziliaya, in quihualmotepotztoquiliaya.
Auh in yèhuatl in Iuan Diego canel ye huel oquimoçenmacatzino
in ilhuicac Çihuapilli, in içihuatecuiyotzin, auh huel quitequipa-
choaya, inic huèca quitzticatca in ichan, in ialtepeuh, inic huel
ceçemilhuitl quimotlayecoltiliz, quimotlàtlachpanililiz, yèica quimotlatlauhtili in Tlàtohuani Obispo ma canà caltechtzinco in inahuac iteòcaltzin, inic huel oncan yez, quimotlayecoltiliz;[1] auh
quimohuelcaquilili in itlaìtlaniliz; auh niman quimomaquilì cal-
tzintli, in inahuac iteòcaltzin ilhuicac Çihuapilli: canel huel çenca
quimotlaçòtiliaya in Tlàtohuani Obispo.

Niman ic hualmìquani quitlalcahui in ialtepeuh quihualcahuilì-
tehuac in iTlatzin Iuan Bernardino in ical, in itlal, oncan çeçemilhuitl tlateomatia, quimotlàtlachpanililiaya in ilhuicac Çihuapilli,
ixpantzinco mopechtecaya, quimotlaocolnonochiliaya, ihuan à-
mo huècauhtica in moyolcuitiaya, tlaçeliaya, moçahuaya, tlamà-
çehuaya, mohuitequia, tepozmatlatl tequàqua[2] ic mocuitlalpiaya,
xomolli, caltechtli quitocaya[3] inic huel iyoca izçā içel quimo-
macaz in tlatlatlauhtiliztli inic quimononochilitiez in ilhuicac
Çihuapilli. Icnooquichtli catca, oc yuh òxihuitl[4] quimottititzinoz
izçenquizcaIchpochtzintli in omomiquilì in içihuahuàtzin[5] catca
itoca Maria Lucia; auh inehuan chipahuacanenque, mopixque[6]
mochpochmiquilì in içihuauh, no yèhuatl telpochnen, aic quiximà çihuatl yèica çeppa quicacque in itemachtiltzin Fray Toribio
Motolinia çemè in màtlactin onmomen San Francisco Teopixque
huel yancuican màxitico; in quenin huel çenca quimohuellamach-

---

[1]*Ma canà ... quimotlayecoltiliz.* Somewhat more literally, the passage
seems to say "let there be somewhere by a wall near her temple in order for
him to be able to be there and serve her."

[2]*Tepozmatlatl tequàqua*: i.e., a cilice.

[3]*Xomolli caltechtli quitocaya.* Molina glosses this phrase (cast in the
reverential) as "to hide," and in another place as "to take shelter in the shade"
(VM, Nahuatl/Span., f. 161; Span./Nahuatl, f. 10).

Lady, our precious mother of Guadalupe, so that she might look
after his soul. He made an offering to her, as appears in his will
at the very beginning of the statement he ordered, which was
done on the second day of March in the year 1563.

ONCE THE consummate Virgin, the heavenly Lady of Guadalupe, was in her precious home, she worked many and innumerable miracles, with which she befriended the local people and
the Spaniards, and all the different peoples who called on and
followed her. As for Juan Diego, since he had dedicated himself
entirely to the heavenly Lady as his patron, it concerned him
very much that her home was too far away from his altepetl for
him to be able to serve her and sweep up for her each day. For
that reason he begged the lord bishop that he could stay somewhere by a wall near her temple in order to serve her.[1] He approved his request and gave him a small house near the temple
of the heavenly Lady, for the lord bishop esteemed him very
highly.

Thereupon he moved and abandoned his altepetl; on departing
he left his house and land to his uncle Juan Bernardino. There
[at Tepeyacac] he used to devote himself daily to spiritual things;
he would sweep for the heavenly Lady, prostrate himself before
her, and sorrowfully invoke her. He would frequently go to
confession and communion, fast, do penance, punish himself,
and gird himself with a sharp metal net.[2] He would search out a
remote corner[3] so that very much apart, all by himself, he could
give himself to prayer and converse with the heavenly Lady. He
was a widower; two years before the consummate Virgin appeared to him, his wife, whose name was María Lucía, died.
They lived together in purity; they kept themselves chaste.[6] His
wife died a virgin. He too lived as a virgin; he never knew a
woman, for once they had heard a sermon of fray Toribio
Motolinia, one of the twelve friars of Saint Francis who were the

---

[4]*Òxihuitl*: for *ōxihuitl*.

[5]*Içihuahuàtzin*: although it appears at first glance incorrect, this form is
quite often seen in texts, including those of well versed writers. The *-huà-* is
apparently an older, fuller version of the possessive ending usually occurring
as *-uh*, here preserved because of its protected internal position.

[6]*Mopixque*: see the related forms under "casta persona" and "castidad" in
VM, Span./Nahuatl, f. 25v.

tilia in Teotl Dios, ihuan in itlaçòmahuizNantzin in chipahua-
canemiliztli, in nepializtli. Auh in quexquich quimìtlanililìaya,[1]
inic quimotlatlauhtiliaya in ilhuicac Çihuapilli, moch quimonel-
tililiaya; no yuhq̃ in aquìque itech mocahuaya, ca inpãpa[2] quimo-
màçehuiaya in tlein intlanequiliz, inchoquiz, intlaocol.

Auh in iTlatzin in Iuan Bernardino in quittac in huel çẽca qui-
motlayecoltilia in toTecuiyo, yhuan in itlaçònantzin, quihual-
tocazquia, inic nehuã yezquia: auh àmo quinec quilhui inic monequia izçan ompa yez in ichan inic quipixtiyez in incal, in intlal
quincahuilitiàque intàhuan, incolhuan; yèica ca yuh quimonahuatili in ilhuicac Çihuapilli inic çan içel yez. Auh in ipan xihuitl mil
y quinientos y quarenta y quatro años momanaco in huey
cocoliztli, auh itech motlali in Iuan Bernardino; auh in ye huellanauhtoc quimocochittili in ilhuicac, Çihuapilli quimolhuili inic
ye inman in ye oncan ic miquiz, ma moyollali, macamo quen
mochihua in iyollo ca quimomanahuiliz in imiquiztempan, qui-
mohuiquiliz in ompa itlàtocachantzinco ilhuicac; canel çemìcac
itechtzinco omopouh, omotzatzili, huel ipan caxtolilhuitl Mayo in
ipan xihuitl omoteneuh in momiquili, auh oncan hualhuicoc in
Tepeiacac inic oncan tococ in ìtic iteòcaltzin in ilhuicac Çihuapilli, auh ca yuh itencopatzinco mochiuh in Obispo, auh ca
quipiaya nauhpohualli ihuan chiquaçenxihuitl in ìquac momiquilì.

Auh izçatepan in Iuan Diego ye yuh caxtolli ozçe xihuitl in
oncan quimotequipanilhuia, in ilhuicac Çihuapilli in momiqui-
lico, huel ipan in xihuitl mill y quinientos y quarenta y ocho;
huel ìquac in momiquilì Tlàtohuani Obispo. Auh in ye inman in
ye oncan çenca quimoyollalili in ilhuicac Çihuapilli, huel quimottili; quimolhuili inic ye inman in quimàçehuatiuh in quimo-
tlamachtitiuh in ompa in ilhuicac, in ixquich in oquimotenehuili-
li, auh no oncan motocac iteopanchantzinco, auh ye yuh èpo-
hualli onmàtlactli ihuã nahui xiuhtia in momiquilì, in quimohuiquili izçenquizcaichpochtzintli, ihuan in itlaçòconetzin in iyolia in
ianima in ompa quimoçentlamachtia in ilhuicac pàpaquiliztli: ma
yuh quimonequiltitzino inic no tehuã tictotlayecoltilizque, tic-

---

[1]*Quimìtlanililìaya*: the second *i* marked with a grave accent is short and
not followed by glottal stop.

[2]*Inpãpa*: probably for *ipãpa* or *in ipãpa*. If we should take the form as

very first to arrive, on how much a pure life and chastity please God the deity and his precious, revered mother. And whatever he would ask her for, when he prayed to the heavenly Lady, she would grant it all. Likewise, all those who would leave themselves to her would obtain on her account[2] whatever was their wish, the object of their tears and sorrow.

When his uncle Juan Bernardino saw how very greatly he was serving our Lord and his precious mother, he was going to follow him so that the two might be together. But he [Juan Diego] refused; he said that it was necessary that he [Juan Bernardino] just be at his home in order to take care of their houses and lands that their forebears had left them, because the heavenly Lady commanded him to be all alone. In the year 1544 a great epidemic broke out. It came upon Juan Bernardino, and when he lay gravely ill, he saw the heavenly Lady in a dream. She told him that it was time for him to die, that he should be consoled, that his heart should not be troubled, that she would come to defend him when he was at the point of death, and that she would take him to her royal home in heaven, since he had always dedicated himself to her and invoked her. It was exactly on the fifteenth day of May in the aforesaid year that he died. He was taken to Tepeyacac to be buried inside the temple of the heavenly Lady; it was done in this way by order of the bishop. He was eighty-six years old when he died.

LATER, AFTER Juan Diego had served the heavenly Lady there for sixteen years, he died, exactly in the year of 1548; it was just then that the lord bishop died. When it was time, the heavenly Lady greatly consoled him. He was able to see her; she told him that the time had arrived for him to go attain and enjoy in heaven everything that she had promised him. He too was buried in her churchly home. He was seventy-four years old when he died, when the consummate Virgin and her precious child took his soul to where it would enjoy completely the happiness of heaven. May it be her wish that we too may serve her and abandon all the worldly things that lead us astray, so that we too may attain the eternal riches of heaven. Amen.

---

correct, the translation would have to be "she would obtain for the sake of those who would leave themselves to her whatever was their wish . . ."

tlalcahuizque, in ixquich tlalticpacayotl in tetlapololti inic no huel
tictomàcehuizque in ilhuicac çemìcac necuiltonolli. Ma iuh mochihua.

NICAN tlantica in ittoloca, in ipohualoca in huei tlamahuiçolli, inic omonexiti in ixiptlatzin in ilhuicac TlatòcaÇihuapilli, Totlaçòmahuiznantzin Guadalupe: ihuan in quezquitlamantli
in omìcuilo, itlamahuiçoltzin, in oquihualmochihuilìtia, ic qui-
monextili in itepalehuiliztzin intechcacopa in itechpatzinco omo-
tzàtzilìque, oquimotemachìtzinòque;[1] auh ca çenca miec in omocauh,[2] in oquipolò in cahuitl, in aoc mà aca quilnamiqui inic àmo
oquimocuitlahuìq̃ in huehuetq̃ in ma quimìcuilhuiani niman in
ìquac mochiuh. Auh ca yeppa yuhque in tlalticpac tlaca, izçan
huel ìquac, quimahuiztilia, quitlaçòcamati in iteicneliltzin ilhuicac
TlatòcaÇihuapilli, intla oquimomàçehuìque, auh in moztla, in
huiptla ca ye intlalcahualizpan contlaztihui inic aocmo inpan
hualàçi, izçatepan hualhui, quihualmomàçehuia in itlanextzin, in
itonatiuhtzin Totecuiyo. Auh ca huel ye yèhuatl in, in ipampa
achi opoliuhca, omolcauhca in iteicneliltzin ilhuicac Çihuapilli,
inic çenca huei tlamahuiçoltica omonexiti in nican ichantzinco
Tepeyacac; inic àmo çenca in iuh monequia quihualmomachiltia,
quihualmocuitìtzinoa in imaçehualtzitzinhuā in huel inpampa oncan omocaltìtzino inic oncan quinmocaquiliz in innetoliniliz, in
inpatzmiquiliz, in inchoquiz, in intlaìtlaniliz, auh quinmomaquiliz, quinmocneliliz in itepalehuiliztzin; in iuh ye omìtto yèhuatzin
quimolhuili, quimomaquili in itlàtoltzin in imaçehualtzin Iuan
Diego in quimottitìtzino. Auh inic àmo çenmochi tlamiz, quipòpoloz in cahuitl in itlamahuiçoltzin ilhuicac tlatòcaÇihuapilli,
ca oquimotlaçònequilti[3] itepalehuilizticatzinco motlilanaz,[4] mote-

---

[1]*Oquimotemachìtzinòque*: in this instance, as in that of a similar verb
stem above (at n. 6, pp. 64–65), the meaning, "trust in her," is quite clear.
Nevertheless, the verb again does not behave according to dictionary norms.
Temachia standardly takes either a specific object prefix or a reflexive prefix,
but not both (VM, Nahuatl/ Span., f. 96v). The writer here apparently
thinks that both are necessary, so much so that he resorts to the *-tzinoa*
reverential (the reflexive-plus-applicative reverential cannot be used when the
reflexive has semantic significance, because the reflexive prefix cannot be
doubled). The present case does not help in the interpretation of the one
above; both are deviant from the known norm, but they do not agree with
each other. It does, however, agree with an almost identical instance below

HERE ends the story and account of the great miracle by which the image of the heavenly Queen, our precious revered mother of Guadalupe, appeared, and of some of her miracles that were written down, which she came to do, by which she manifested her aid toward those who called upon her and put their trust in her.[1] But a great deal has been left out,[2] which time has erased and no one at all remembers any more, because the ancients did not take care to write it down when it happened. The people of the world have always been like that; only at the very moment when they have obtained them do they wonder at and give thanks for the favors of the heavenly Queen, but soon they cast them into oblivion, so that those who come afterward in attaining the light of the sun of our Lord arrive too late for them. This is the very reason why the benevolence of the heavenly Lady by which she very miraculously appeared here in her home at Tepeyacac had rather disappeared [from people's minds] and been forgotten, since her humble subjects have not made it known or acknowledged it as much as was needed—her humble subjects for whose very sake she built her house there so that in it she might hear their afflictions, their grief, their tears, and their entreaties, and she might give them and grant them the favor of her aid. As was said above, she spoke and gave her word to her humble subject Juan Diego to whom she revealed herself. In order that everything should not perish and that time should not erase the miracles of the heavenly Queen, she lovingly saw fit that, with her help, it should be written and

---

at n. 3, pp. 118–19.

[2]*Omocauh.* This form, the verb *cahua* ("to leave, abandon," etc.) in the preterit reflexive, stands in close connection with the verb *poloa* immediately following; a few lines below, the related verb *polihui* is similarly connected with a form of the verb *ilcahua*, "to forget." In the preterit reflexive, only a single letter differentiates the two; one must wonder if the intention here was not *omolcauh*, "it was forgotten."

[3]*Oquimotlaçònequilti*: because of a smudge in the copy of the original we used, the *n* in this form cannot be seen clearly.

[4]*Motlilanaz*: based on an unattested verb; see n. 1, p. 54.

pozpachoz in onez, in omopantlaz, maçihui ohuìtica in omo-
neltili, inic çennohuian tepan àçitiuh motemachiltitiuh.[1]

Auh in maçihui ye huel nelli yuhqui ca çan çentetzintli in ilhuicac
Tlaçòçihuapilli içeltlaçònantzin[2] in Dios itlaçòpiltzin, izçan içeltzin çennohuian çemanahuac tictomahuiztililia in titlaneltoca-
catzitzinhuan itlaçòconetzin; ma huel yuh ye in imix, in inyollo
tlalticpac tlaca, càmo çan quezquican inic çennohuian altepepã,
huel yèhuatzin in oquimopèpeni, oquimixquechili, in iyeyantzin,
ihuan in ixiptlatzin inic oncan quinmopalehuiliz in icnotlaca in
ixpãtzinco huallazque, quihualmotemachìtzinòtiazque[3] çenmoch
ica in inyollo, quimìtlanililizque in itecanechihualiztzin.[4] In iuh
ye izquican quimochihuilia in nican totlalpan Nueua España: ca
in itlaçòixiptlatzin in quinhualmohuicalti Caxtilteca yancuican
calaquico, teyaochihuilico, ye machizti in quen mochiuh inic
çeme yèhuantin in yaotequipanèque[5] quimotlatilìtiquiz in oncan
totoltepec in ìquac Mexìca yaotica quinquixtìque, quintòtocaque
Mexìco in Españolestin: auh ca oncan huècauhtica mèmetla
mopolihuitìticatca ixquichca çe maçehualtzintli, quimottiti, quimonànahuatili, oncan quimocaltiliz in iuh ye omìtto. Auh in
ixquich itepalehuiliztzin in quimochihuilia, in ye quimoteicnelilia
in oncan ic moyetztica, ca çenca huel miec in oquimàceuhque in
nepapan tlaca, ilhuice yèhuantin in Caxtilteca in oquihualmo-
huiquilìque, ihuan quimotlatequipanilhuililia[6] in ichantzinco.

---

[1]*Motemachiltitiuh*. It was seen above at n. 6, pp. 64–65, that the writer
sometimes (not always) proceeds as if he thinks that *temachia*, "to trust," is
intransitive. The present form is consonant with that interpretation, though
it uses a causative rather than an applicative suffix to complete the reverential. Yet the "trust" sense does not fit the context as readily here as in the
other case. Siméon (DS, p. 217) lists an infrequently seen intransitive verb
machia, "to be known"; our form, however, has a -*te*- which cannot be
accounted for if this *machia* is the base. If the intention is *temachia*, the
form (which in standard grammar would be *motemachitiuh*) would mean "it
is gaining confidence [from the public]." *Momachiltitiuh* would mean "it is
becoming known." The "known" sense is so appropriate and pairs so well
with the just preceding verb that we have provisionally chosen it as the
possible intention.

[2]*Iceltlaçonantzin*. This is an unusual, even an incorrect form. *Icel*,
"alone, only, sole, by oneself," is a self-contained expression; a following
noun would normally be in the absolutive, as in *icel conetl*, "only child"
(see VM, Nahuatl/Span., f. 10), or if possessed would have its own
possessive prefix. Here the *i*- of *icel* is made to serve as prefix of the noun

printed, so that when it had appeared and been published—and though with difficulty it has been realized—absolutely everywhere it would be reaching people [and becoming known?].[1]

Granted that it is very true that the heavenly precious Lady, the only precious mother[2] of God's precious child, is a single thing, and we believers in her precious child honor her alone everywhere in the world, let the people of the earth realize that in many places in the altepetls all around she herself has chosen out and set up her dwelling places and her images so that there she may help the needy who should come into her presence trusting in her[3] and asking with all their hearts for her succor.[4] So she has done in many places here in our land of New Spain. For her precious image came along with the Spaniards when they first entered and came to make war. It is well known how it happened that one of the warriors[5] hid it at Totoltepec when passing through at the time when the Mexica by war ejected and drove the Spaniards out of Mexico. For a long time it was lost there among the magueyes, until she revealed herself to a poor commoner and directed him to build her a house there, as was said before. And where she is, different people have obtained very, very much of the aid she provides and has dispensed, especially the Spaniards, who brought her and serve her in her

---

as well. Moreover, *ltl* is a forbidden sequence in a Nahuatl word, automatically becoming *ll*. One would have expected *icel itlaçònantzin.*

[3]*Quihualmotemachìtzinòtiazque.* See n. 1, pp. 116–17.

[4]*Itecanechihualiztzin*: derived from *teca ninochihua*, "to care for or succor someone" (AC, f. 19v).

[5]*Yaotequipanòque*: probably intended as an equivalent for Spanish *soldados*, "soldiers," as the later generations of Spaniards called the conquerors.

[6]*Quimotlatequipanilhuililia.* Strictly speaking, this form has one *li* too many. "To work or do service" is *tlatequipanoa*; "to serve someone" is *tetlatequipanilhuia* with an applicative (metathesized as usual with an *-oa* verb) and a personal object; the reverential thereof is *motetlatequipanilhuilia*, with only one *li*. The present form has three applicatives where only two are called for. Nevertheless, an apparently extra *li* does sometimes slip into elevated Nahuatl texts. Some have a basis in variant or older forms. Thus above in the text there appears *itlapopolhuililoca*, "his pardon," with one *li* more than usually seen. It is justified, however; Molina gives the verb "to pardon" not only as *tlapopolhuia*, but also as *tlapopolhuilia* (VM, Nahuatl/ Span., f. 132v). In the present text, the *-huilia* form is used several times, in both the verb and derived forms; the shorter form also appears once.

Auh in ompa totonqui tlalpan, ihualquiçayanpa in tonatiuh, oncan in hualàci huei Acalli, itentla in poyec atl, in teoatl itocayòcan
Coçamalloapan, oc centetzintli mehuiltìtica itlaçòixiptlatzin ilhuicac tlàtocaÇihuapilli, izçenca huey tlamahuiçolli quimochihuili
inic oncan mehuiltìtica, ihuan inic quinmopalehuilia in ixquichtin
quimonochilia, quimotzatzìlilia[1] in innetolinilizpan. Çanno yuhcatzintli in mehuiltìtica in itocayòcan Temazcaltzinco; ihuan oc
quezquican altepepã.

Ilhuice yèhuatzin in itechpatzinco tontlatòtihui in nican Tepeyacac quimixquechili in iyeyantzin, ihuan quimotemaquili in ixiptlatzin huei tlamahuiçoltica, in àmo aca tlalticpac tlacatl tlàcui-
lòcatzintli, oquimochihuili, oquimotlapalaquilì, ca huel yèhuatzin
in omocopintzino inic oquimotlaçonequilti oncan mehuiltìtiez.
Auh in maçihui çenmochintin ye quinmopalehuilia in nepapan
tlaca in innetolinalizpan[2] quihualmotlàpalhuia in ichantzinco. Ma
huel yuh ye in imix, in inyollo in nican tlaca maçehualtzitzintin,
ca huel yèhuantin in inpampa oquimotlaçonequilti in inÇihuapil-
latòcatzin oncan mocaltitzinoz. Auh ca ye nelli yuhqui, càmo çan
nen, çan tlapic in huel niman ipeuhyan tlaneltoquiliztli, omentin
maçehualtzitzintin quinmottititzino in ayà[3] ixtomi, in ayà[3] ixquich
ic impan tlaneci, ic impan tlatlalchipahua in tlaneltoquiliztli, inic
cenca oquimonextili ca huel yèhuantin in quinmotemolico, ca
oquihualmotlaçònequiltitzinòtia, in ma quimoÇihuapillatòcatì-
tzinocan, in ma quimomahuiztililìtzinocã, in ma quimotlatequipanilhuililican[4] inic içehuallotitlantzinco quinmaniliz quinmo-
maquilìtiez in imatzin, in itepalehuiliztzin. Canel àmo mopoli-
huitiaya in ìquac on in mahuiztique tlaca, ihuan in Tlaçòteopixque in ye huècauhtica itetequipanòcatzitzinhuan ilhuicac tlatòca-
Çihuapilli; auh àmo çeme yèhuãtin quimotlaçòicnelili inic quimottititzinoz, ca çan inceltin in maçehualtzitzintin in tlayohuayan,
mixtecomac actoya in oc nòma quintlaçòtlaya quintequipanoaya
in iztlacateototontin izçan tlamachihualtin ixiptlahuan in toyauh[5]
in tlacatecolotl, maçihui ye innacazpan ohualàcica in tlaneltoquiliztli ixquichca in quicacque, inic omoteittìtìtzino in itlaçòmahuiznantzin totecuiyo Xp̄o,[6] ihuan inic oquittaque oquimahuiçòque

---

[1]*Quimotzatzìlilia*: for *quimotzàtzililia*.

[2]*Innetolinalizpan*: for *innetolinilizpan*.

[3]*Ayà*: the *à* is short and not followed by glottal stop. In any case, *ayamo*
is much more frequent in this sense, and the short form is usually *aye*.

[4]*Quimotlatequipanilhuililican*: contains the same extra *li* as the example

home. In the hot lands in the east, where the great boats arrive, on the shore of the salt water, the ocean, at the place called Coçamalloapan, there resides another precious image of the heavenly Queen, who worked a great miracle in order to reside there and aid all who call on her and invoke her in their afflictions. Also similar is the one that resides in the place called Temazcaltzinco, and [the ones] in some other altepetls.

Especially she about whom we are speaking set up her residence here at Tepeyacac and by a great miracle gave people her image, which no earthly human artist made or colored. It was she herself who made her own copy, because she lovingly saw fit to make her residence there. Although she now helps all different kinds of people who in their affliction come to greet her in her home, let the local people, the humble commoners, be sure that it was for their very sake that their Queen condescended to house herself there. Indeed, it was not vainly or for nothing that right when the Christian faith was just getting a start, she revealed herself to two humble commoners who had not yet opened their eyes, on whom the faith had not yet fully shone or dawned, in order to make very clear that it was precisely for them that she came searching, that she came lovingly desiring that they take her for their Queen, that they might revere and serve her, so that she might take them in her protective shadow and be giving them her helping hand. For in that time there was no lack of respected people and precious friars who had long been servants of the heavenly Queen, and she did not grant any of them the favor of revealing herself to him, but only to the humble commoners who were submerged in night and darkness, and even though the faith had already reached their ears, they were still cherishing and serving the false little gods that were only hand-made images of our enemy, the demon, until the time that they heard that the precious revered mother of Christ our Lord[5] had revealed herself and that they saw and wondered at her image, an absolute marvel in the way it takes on a human

---

above commented on in n. 6, pp. 118–19.

[5]*Toyauh*: standard *toyaouh*.

[6]*Xp̄o*. It was quite rare at this time, in either Nahuatl or Spanish, for any occurrence of the word *Cristo* (*Xp̄o*) not to be preceded by *Jesu*. The latter word may have been inadvertently omitted.

in ixiptlatzin, cenquizcamahuizticatzintli inic motlacanexitìtica.¹
Ca çenca ic oixtonquè, otlachixque, yuhquin impan otlathui-
tiquiz. Auh (in iuh quìcuilòtehuaque in huehuetque) niman
çequintin in Pipiltin, çanno yuhque in intlahuicalhuan maçehualtzitzintin izçenyollocacopa quintlazque quintepeuhque, quiyahuac quinquixtìque in ixiptlahuan tlacatecolotl; peuhque ye ic
quimomahuiztililia, quimoneltoquitìtzinoa in toTecuiyo IESV
Christo, yhuan in itlaçònantzin. Inic onnelti càmo çaniyo ic
ohualmohuicac, omoteittitzinoco in ilhuicac tlatòcaÇihuapilli
toTlaçònantzin Guadalupe inic quinmopalehuiz² macehualtzitzintin ytechcacopa in intlalticpacnetolinaliz³ ca oc çenca oquihual-
melehuilìtia quinmomaquiliz in itlanextzin, in itepalehuiliztzin
inic quimiximachilizque in huel nelli iceltzin Teotl Dios, ihuan
inic ipaltzinco quittazque, quiximatizque in ilhuicac nemiliztli.
Auh inic yuh quimochihuilì in, ca ipan àci, huel yèhuatzin qui-
mocalaquilico, quimotlachicahuililico in tlaneltoquiliztli ye oqui-
mopehualtilìca quimotemaquilia in itlaçòpilhuantzitzin San Francisco inic otòtococ in tlateotoquiliztli, tlalpan huicoc oxitin in
itlàtocayo immoteomachtlanini Tlacatecolotl in tlayohuayan, in
mixtecomac oquinnemiti in itlachihualtzitzinhuan, in imaçe-
hualtzitzinhuan toTecuiyo izçenca oquimixtepetlatilìca inic yèhuatl quimacazque in teomahuiçotl, in teòcalli, in teomomoztli,⁴
in xochitl, in copalli, in intolol,⁵ in intlanqua,⁶ in innepechte-
quiliz, izçan huel içeltzin inemactzin in ilhuicac mehuiltìtica, in
otechmochihuili. Auh ca yeppa itequitzin in ilhuicac tlatòca-
Çihuapilli in quimoxitiniliz, in quimopòpolhuiz in tlateotoquiliztli
in iuh quimolhuilia, in iuh itechcacopatzinco quimocuitìtzinoa in
tonantzin Sāta Iglesia, in izquipa quimotlatlauhtilia, quimoyec-
tenehuilia, quimolhuilìtzinoa, *Gaude Maria Virgo cunctas here-
ses sola interemisti in vniuerso mundo,*⁷ in quìttoznequi, ma

---

¹*Motlacanexitìtica*: based on the verb *tlacaneci*, "to seem human," which
meaning can be deduced not only from its constituent roots but from a
negative phrasing in Molina (VM, Nahuatl/Span., f. 115v).

²*Quinmopalehuiz*: standard *quinmopalehuìliz*.

³*Intlalticpacnetolinaliz*: for *intlalticpacnetoliniliz*.

⁴*Teomomoztli*. In addition to meaning altar or platform in the preconquest style, *momoztli* can also refer to a small temple or chapel in the
countryside (VM, Nahuatl/Span., f. 115v).

⁵*Intolol*. The intransitive verb *toloa*, "to lower or bend the head," could

aspect.[1] At this they opened their eyes wide, they saw, as if the dawn had come upon them. Then (as the ancients left written) some nobles, and likewise their followers the humble commoners, with all their hearts cast away, hurled down, and threw out the images of the demon. With that they began to revere and believe in our Lord Jesus Christ and his precious mother. Thus is verified that not only did the heavenly Queen, our precious mother of Guadalupe, come here to reveal herself in order to aid the humble commoners in their earthly afflictions, she wanted even more to give them her light and aid so that they would recognize the one true deity, God, and through him see and know the heavenly life.

As to how she did this, she arrived at that time, she herself came to introduce and fortify the faith, which the precious children of Saint Francis had already begun to impart to people, so that idolatry was banished and thrown down, and the rule of the demon collapsed, of him who wishes to be taken for a god, who caused our Lord's creatures, his humble subjects, to live in night and darkness, blinding them so much that they would give him divine honor, temples, divine altars,[4] flowers and incense, bowing of the head,[5] kneeling,[5] and deep obeisance, which are the due of him alone who dwells in heaven, who made us. It has always been the task of the heavenly Queen to destroy and wipe out idolatry, as our holy mother church says and acknowledges in her regard, whenever she prays to her, praises her, and says to her, *Gaude Maria Virgo cunctas haereses sola interemisti in universo mundo,*[7] which means, "Rejoice, ever

---

well lead to a patientive noun *tololli,* which would mean the result of that action, and could be taken to refer to a bow of the head. Such a word is not attested to our knowledge, however, and the normal noun for bowing the head is *tololiztli.* Here one would have expected *intololiz.*

[6]*Intlanqua.* This means literally "their knees." Perhaps it makes a metaphorical pair with *intolol.* Again, however, one would have expected *innetlanquaquetzaliz,* "their kneeling" (see VM, Span./Nahuatl, f. 14).

[7]Latin: "Rejoice, O Virgin Mary, you alone have destroyed all heresies throughout the world." From the office of the Blessed Virgin Mary.

ximopaquiltitie çemìcac ichpochtzintlè Santa Mariatzinè[1] izçennohuian tlalticpac moçeltzin oticmopòpolhui, oticmàtletilili in
ixquich in tlateotoquiliztli, ihuan in chicotlaneltoquiliztli.
Auh in maçihui ye nelli yuhqui, ca huel oneltico in nican totlalpan Nueua España inic çenca monequi in ma ìçacan in ma
ixtomican in iz tlaca in maçehualtzitzintin in quittazque in quipohuaz[2] in nican omìcuilo in inpampa oquimochihuili in ilhuicac
tlaçòÇihuapilli, inic quinemilizque catlèhuatl monequi in quichi-
huazque inic quimocuepililizque, quimoxtlahuililizq̃ in itetlaçòtlaliztzin, inic no tehuan quimàcehuazq̃ in itepalehuiliztzin in ìquac
quimonochilizque noce intla ichantzinco quihualmotlàpalhuiz-
que, quihualmottilizq̃ in itlaçòmahuizixiptlayotzin, ca quimoneltililiz in itlàtoltzin inic oncã oquimotlaçònequilti mocaltìtzinoz
inic quinmopalehuiliz in maçehualtzitzintin. Ma tlacahua in iyec-
yollotzin in toTlaçòmahuiznantzin ma yèhuatzin quimocuetlanili
in toyollo, inic toçenyollo ica tictomahuiztililizque in nican tlalticpac ixquichca inic itepalehuilizticatzinco tixtelolotica tictottiliz-
que in ompa in inecuiltonolizyeyantzinco. Ma iuh mochihua. —

L A V S   D E O.

---

[1] *Çemìcac ichpochtzintlè Santa Mariatzinè*. These phrases are in the masculine version of the vocative, which is incorrect if "our mother the Holy
Church" is still speaking. Probably the writer had lost the thread and was

Virgin Saint Mary,[1] who alone have destroyed and annihilated all idolatry and perverse belief over the entire earth."

Granted that this is so, it was fully verified here in our land of New Spain, so that it is very necessary for the local people, the humble commoners, to awaken and open their eyes to see and read what has been written here that the heavenly precious Lady did for their sake, in order to consider what they need to do to return and pay back her love for people and along with others attain her aid when they call upon her, or if they come to her home to greet her and see her precious, revered image. She will keep her word, because she lovingly wished her home to be built there in order to help the humble commoners. May our precious revered mother grant that she inflame our hearts so that we may honor her with all our heart here on earth until that time when by her aid we will see her with our eyes in her fortunate dwelling place. Amen.

Laus Deo.

viewing the translation simply as an abstract statement, or as though uttered by himself.

[2]*Quipohuaz*: for *quipohuazque*.

TLATLATLAVHTILIZTLI, IC MOTLATLAVH-
tìtzinoz in ilhuicac tlatòcaÇihuapilli toTlaçònantzin
Guadalupe.

*

ILHVICAC TlatòcaÇihuapillè, çemìcac tlateochihualIchpochtzintlè
Tlatlacatzintlè, ma ximopaquiltitie in titlaçòichpotzin[1] in Dios te-
Tatzin. Ma ximopaquiltìtie in titlaçòNantzin in Dios itlaçòPiltzin.
Ma ximopaquiltìtie in titlaçòNamictzin in Dios Espiritu Santo Tèhuatzin in timitzontoyectenehuilia in ilhuicac otihualmotemohui,
auh cenca huei tlamahuiçoltica otiquinmottitìtzinoco in icnomace-
hualtzitzintin. Tèhuatzin timitzõtotzàtzililia, in titotlaçòmahuiz-
Nantzin Guadalupe, in çenca huey teicnoittaliztica otitechmoma-
quilìtia in mixiptlayotzin in ixpantzinco titotzàtzilizque in ticno-
tlaca in tlaiyohuilizpan tinemì in itlalticpactzinco motlaçòconetzin:
Ma tohuicpa xichualmocuepili in mixtelolotzin, macamo ic ti-
mitztotlàeltilican in ixquich in totlàtlacol. Ça ye xicmoneltilili in
motlàtoltzin inic titechmopalehuiliz inic topan timehuitìtzìnoz;[2]
ma ticmàcehuacan in motlanextzin inic tiquittazque in ilhuicac
nemiliztli. Auh in ixquich inic otictotlapilchihuililìque, otictotla-
tlacalhuililìq̃[3] in toTecuiyo: ma mopampatzinco tipòpolhuililocan,
ma tèhuatzin xicmoçehuili in iyollotzin in motlaçòconetzin, ma
ixquich ma[4] onçeçehui in itlahueltzin, in iquallantzin,[5] ma tech-
mocnoittili in titlachihualtzitzinhuan in mocehuellotitlantzinco[6]
tonacticate in timitzontotzàtzililia in axcã; auh in ye oncan in to-
miquiliztempan ma xicmìquanili, ma xicmotòtoquili in toyaouh,
in totetlapololtìcauh, inic paca,[7] yocoxca mocenmactzinco
mantiaz in toyolia in tanima, inic ixpantzinco neçi-
tiuh in itechiuhcatzin Dios. Ma
iuh mochihua.
I E S V S.
(†)

---

[1]*Titlaçòichpotzin.* Because of weakening in speech, *ch* could be omitted
before *tz* even in the strictest tradition of ecclesiastical Nahuatl writing; the
form is equivalent to *titlaçòichpochtzin.* Except for this instance, however,
the fuller form is used throughout the text. (Four cases of a comparable sim-
plification of *tztz* to *tz* do occur).

[2]*Topan timehuitìtzinoz*: based on *tepan ehua*, "to favor, succoring another in some danger" (VM, Span./Nahuatl, f. 62; Nahuatl/Span., f. 102).

[3]*Otictotlatlacalhuililiq̃.* This is based on *itlacoa*, "to do something wrong
or badly, do damage, sin." The applicative is *itlacalhuia*, whose reverential

PRAYER TO BE DIRECTED
to the heavenly Queen, our precious mother
of Guadalupe.

*

REJOICE, heavenly Queen , eternally blessed Virgin, O merciful one, rejoice, you who are the precious daughter of God the Father. Rejoice, you who are the precious mother of God's precious child. Rejoice, you who are the precious spouse of God the Holy Spirit. It is you we praise, you who have descended from heaven and by a very great miracle have come to reveal yourself to the poor humble commoners. To you we cry, you who are our precious revered mother of Guadalupe, you who in your very great compassion gave us your image, before which we wretches who live in pain on your precious child's earth cry out. Turn your eyes toward us here; may we not disgust you with all our sins. Rather, keep your word to help us and favor us in our difficulties.[2] May we attain your light in order to see the life in heaven. And for your sake may we be pardoned all our sins and offenses against our Lord. May you appease the heart of your precious child; may all his wrath and anger subside. May you take pity on us who are his creatures, who are under your protective shade, who cry out to you today. And then at the time of our death please remove and put to flight our foe, who leads us astray, so that happily and peacefully our souls may go to lie entirely in your hands, so that they may go appear in the presence of God, their creator. Amen.
JESUS.
(†)

---

has a reflexive prefix and a standard -*lia* applicative suffix. Thus the present form has one *li* too many in the same fashion as *tequipanoa* at n. 6, pp. 118–19. By standard grammar the form should be *otictotlatlacalhuiliq̄*.

[4]*Ma*. An optative phrase does sometimes contain a second, strictly speaking redundant *ma*, but usually at an interval of several nuclear words. Here we are probably dealing with inadvertent repetition.

[5]*Iquallantzin*: standard *iqualantzin*.

[6]*Mocehuellotitlantzinco*: for *mocehuallotitlantzinco*.

[7]*Paca*: standard *pacca*.

Appendix 1:

Comparison of an episode in the *Huei tlamahuiçoltica* and in Miguel Sánchez's *Imagen* in the original languages[1]

El proprio dia boluiò con la Respuesta, y *subiendo al señalado Sitio de aquel Monte*, el Mensagero fide digno, Iuan Diego, hallando à MARIA Virgen, que lo *esperava* piadosa, *Humillandose à su presencia* con todas reverencias *le dixo*.

Obedecî Señora, y Madre mia *tu mandato, no sin trabaxo entrè a visitar al Obispo*, à cuyos pies me arrodillè: *el Piadosamente me recibiò*, Amorosamente me bendixo, Atentamête *me escuchò* y Tibiamente *respondiò diziendome*, Hijo *otro dia* cuando aya lugar *puedes venir, te oyrè mas de espacio* para tu pretension, y *sabrè de raiz aquessa tu embaxada. Iuzguè por* el semblante, y *las palabras, estava persuadido* à que la peticion del *Templo, que tu pides edifique en tu Nombre en aqueste lugar*, nacia de *mi propria imaginacion, y no de tu mandato*, à cuya causa *te suplico encargues* semejante negocio, à otra persona à quien se dè mas credito.

Niman hualmoquep izça ye ìquac ipan çemilhuitl niman *oncã huallamelauh in icpac tepetzintli*, auh ipantzinco àçito in ilhuicac Çihuapilli izçan ye oncan in canin acattopa quimottili, *quimochialitica*; auh in o iuh quimottili *ixpantzinco mopechtecac* motlalchitlaz *quimolhuili*,

notecuiyoè, tlacatlè, Çihuapillè, noxocoyohuè, Nochpochtzinè ca onihuia in ompa otinechmotitlanili, ca *onicneltilito in mìyotzin in motlàtoltzin* maçihui in *ohuìhuitica in onicalac in ompa iyeyean teopixcaTlàtohuani*, ca oniquittac, ca o ixpan nictlali in mìyotzin in motlàtoltzin in yuh otinechmonànahuatili: *onechpaccacelì*, auh *ôquiyeccac*; yece inic *onechnanquili*, yuhquin àmo iyollo ômàcic, àmo monelchihua, *onechilhui oc ceppa tihuallaz, oc ihuiyan nimitzcaquiz*, huel *oc itzinècan niquittaz in tlein ic otihualla* motlayelehuiliz, motlanequiliz. *Huel itech oniquittac in yuh onechnanquili ca momati in moteocaltzin ticmonequiltia mitzmochihuililizã nican àço çan nèhuatl nicyòyocoya, acaçomo motencopatzinco*; ca çenca *nimitznotlatlauhtilia* notecuiyoè, Çihuapillè Noch-

[1]IVM, pp. 80–81; above, pp. 68–71. Translated above, pp. 9–12.

pochtzinè manoço àca çeme in tlaçòpipiltin in iximacho, in ixtilò, in
mahuiztilò *itech xicmocahuili* in
quitquiz, yn quihuicaz in mìiyotzin,
yn motlàtoltzin, *inic neltocoz,* canel
nicnotlapaltzintli, ca nimecapalli, ca
nicacaxtli, ca nicuitlapîlli, ca natlapalli, ca nitco ca nî nimamaloni,
càmo nonènemian, càmo nonèque-
tzayan in ompa tinechmihualia
Nochpochtzinè, Noxocoyohuè, Tlacatlè, Çihuapillè, ma xinechmotla-
pòpolihuili nictequipachoz in mixtzin, in moyollotzin, ipan niyaz,
ipan nihuetziz in moçoma[lt]zin, in
moqualantzin Tlacatlè Notecuiyoè.
Quimonanquilili izçenquizcamahuiz-
ichpochtzintli
tla xiccaqui noxocoyouh ma huel
iuh ye in moyollo càmo tlaçotin in
notetlayecolticahuan in notìtitlanhuan, in huel intech niccahuaz in
quitquizq̃ in nìiyo, in notlàtol, in
quineltilizque in notlanequiliz: yece
huel iuh monequi inic huel tèhuatl
ic tinemiz, ipan titlàtoz, huel *mo-*
matica neltiz mochihuaz, in noçializ, *in notlanequiliz; auh huel ni-*
mitztlatlauhtia noxocoyouh, yhuan
nimitztlaquauhnahuatia ca huel *oc*
çeppa tiaz in moztla tiquittatiuh *in*
Obispo auh *nopampa xicnèmachti,*
huel yuh xiccaquiti in noçializ, in
notlanequiliz, inic quineltiliz *i n*
quichihuaz noteòcal niquìtlanilia,
yhuan huel *oc ceppa xiquilhui in*
quenin huel nèhuatl niçemìcacich-
pochtli Sancta Maria in ninantzin
Teotl Dios in ompa nimitztitlani.
Auh in *Iuan* Diego quimonanquilili,

No faltaràn muchas, *le respondiò la*
Santissima Virgen, mas conviene,
que tu lo solicites, y tenga *por tu*
mano logros en mi desseo, te pido,
encargo, y *ruego,* que *mañana*
buelvas con el mismo cuydado *al*
Obispo, y *de mi parte* otra vez *le*
requieras, y le adviertas mi voluntad
para que se fabrique la casa que le
pido, repitiendole con eficacia, *que*
yo MARIA Virgen, Madre de Dios,
soy la que allà te embio.

Señora mia, *le dixo Juan, con todo*

gusto, cuydado y puntualidad *obe-decerè el orden que me has dado*, por que no entiendas que reuso el trabajo, *el camino*, o cansancio, *no se*

si han de querer oyrme, y quâdo me oigan, si han de determinarse â crerme, yo te verè mañana quando se ponga el Sol, entonces *bolverè con la segunda resolucion del Obispo, yo me voy, quedate en buenas horas.*

quimolhuili

notecuiyoè, Çihuapillè, Nochpoch-tzinè macamo nictequipacho in mix-tzin, in moyollotzin ca *huel noçen-yollocacopa nonyaz noconneltilitiuh in mìîyotzin in motlàtoltzin* ca niman àmo nicnocacahualtia, mano-çe nictecococamati *in òtli* ca nonyaz ca noconchihuatiuh in motlanequi-liztzin, çan huel ye in *àçocàmo ni-yeccacòz; intla noce ye onicacoc àcaçomo nineltocoz*, ca tel *moztla* ye teotlac *in ye oncalaqui tonatiuh, niccuepaquiuh* in mìîyotzin in mo-tlàtoltzin *in tlein ic nechnanquiliz in Teopixcatlatohuani, ca ye nimitzno-tlalcahuilia* noxocoyohuè, Noch-pochtzinè tlacatlè, Çihuapillè, *ma oc ximoçehuitzino*,

Appendix 2:

Translations of excerpts from Miguel Sánchez's
Imagen de la Virgen, 1648

(First apparition)[1]

This City[2] of Mexico having been conquered and having come to terms of peace on the 13th of August of the year 1521, toward the beginning of December of the year of 1531 [the following] occurred in the site that today is called Guadalupe, and originally in the language [of the natives] Tepeyacac, located in view of Mexico City, a league away from it, facing on the north a mountain or hill, rough, stony, and uncultivated, with sufficient height to be able to command a view of all the surrounding area, for if on the south it has the noted city and in the west various settlements, on the east it enjoys a spacious, expansive plain, reaching as far as some lakes of the Indies, all a common passageway to various provinces.

Here one Saturday (it had to be a day consecrated to Mary) an Indian was coming by, who if recently converted, was fortunately aware, for hearing sweet music, well tuned harmonies, heightened counterpoints, and sonorous accents, realizing that it was not nightingales or larks, or any of his familiar birds, chattering sparrows, placid linnets, or celebrated *centzontlis*, he halted in bewilderment and exalted confusion. When that concerted choir or heavenly band composed of angels who had been placed in the open air, using that sacred mountain as a stage, had paused, he heard from that direction a voice calling him by his own name; he was named Juan, with the surname Diego. . . . Juan Diego heard the voice and felt its echoes in his soul, and he began to go around the base of the mountain with his eyes, listen in its recesses, and scrutinize its heights. In the highest place looking to the west he discovered a lady, who commanded him to go up, and so he did.

Once in her presence, astonished without fearing, bewildered without confusion, attentive without fright, he contemplated a beauty that inspired love without danger, a light that illuminated him without leaving him dazzled, an affability that captivated him without flattery. He heard language sweetly pronounced, easy to understand, unforgettably loving—for all this is harbored in the Virgin Mary. She said to him, "Son Juan, where are you going?" . . .

He, pleased and obliged by the tenderness of the words, replied to her,

---

[1]IVM, pp. 76–78.
[2]We have rearranged the paragraphing.

"Lady, I am going to attend the instruction in religious obedience that the friars give us in the settlement of Tlatelolco."

The most holy Mary continued the conversation, revealing and declaring herself to him. "You must know, son, that I am the Virgin Mary, mother of the true God. I want a house, chapel, and temple to be founded for me here, where I can show myself as a compassionate mother to you and yours, to my devotees, to those who should seek me for the relief of their necessities. So that this merciful aim may be achieved, you are to go to the palace of the bishop in Mexico City, and in my name tell him that it is my special will that he construct and build for me a temple on this site, reporting to him what you have attentively heard and devoutly perceived. Go in the assurance that I will generously repay your travail with benefits, your efforts with favors."

Juan humbly worshipped and adored her and obediently hastened and hurried off, for true obedience neither replies in curiosity nor delays in negligence. He proceeded to the city and sought out the episcopal palace, where he found the most illustrious and reverend lord, the first bishop of this holy metropolitan church of Mexico . . . Finally the messenger Juan reached the consecrated prince of the church, don Juan de Zumárraga, with the message of the Virgin Mary.

(Second apparition)[1]

The same day he returned with the reply, and climbing up to the assigned place on that mountain, the trustworthy messenger, Juan Diego, finding the Virgin Mary mercifully awaiting him, humbling himself in her presence with all the forms of reverence said to her, "Lady and Mother, I obeyed your command; not without travail I went in to visit the bishop, at whose feet I knelt down. He received me mercifully, blessed me lovingly, listened to me attentively, and gave a lukewarm answer, saying to me, 'Son, you may come another day when it is appropriate; I will listen to your claim more deliberately, and will get to the root of this mission of yours.' I judged by his appearance and his words that he was persuaded that the petition about the temple that you ask him to build in your name in this place was born of my own imagination and not of your order, for which reason I implore you to charge another person, who will be credited more, with such a matter."

"There will be no lack of many," answered the most holy Virgin, "but it is necessary that you negotiate it and that my desire should succeed at your hands. I ask, charge, and implore you to return tomorrow with the same concern to the bishop and on my behalf to require him and notify him of my

---

[1]IVM, pp. 80–81.

will so that the house I ask of him will be built, repeating to him decidedly that it is I, the Virgin Mary, mother of God, who send you."

"My lady," Juan said to her, "with much pleasure, care, and punctuality I will obey the order you have given me, so that you should not think that I refuse the effort, the road, or the fatigue. I do not know if they will want to hear me, and when they hear me, if they will decide to believe me. I will see you tomorrow when the sun is setting; then I will return with the second decision of the bishop. I am going; I wish you good day."

(Return to the bishop)[2]

Descend now, sacred messenger, and go on your way. So he did, and the following day, Sunday, he attended the morning indoctrination and mass at the church of Santiago in Tlatelolco. Afterwards, at ten o'clock in the morning, he went to the palace of the lord bishop, where with all manner of measures, importuning, and persistence he managed to arrive once again at his feet, wetting them at once with tender tears so that they would be witnesses of the truth and intermediaries of his emotions.

(Third apparition)[3]

At the assigned hour, at sunset, [Juan Diego] arrived at the mountain of Guadalupe with the aid of the Virgin Mary, who was awaiting him . . . He said, "Lady, I repeated my trip, your message, and the visit to the bishop in his palace. For a second time I proposed what you command. I reaffirmed that you sent me; I assured him that you request a house and temple in this place, and that having given you the first reply he sent, you wished me to return. All this with importunings, tears, and sighs, fearing that his angered assistants would give me lashes as too importunate or dismiss me seeing me so stubborn. The bishop, somewhat severely and apparently a bit annoyed, answered me in an unflattering way, saying that [surely I did not expect] that my words, reports, and person alone could move him to an enterprise of such gravity. He examined me curiously about everything I had seen concerning your person and what I had understood of your conduct. I painted you as well as I could with humble reports, I described you with phrases of my small capacity, and I believe that they had an effect, for between dubious and persuaded he decided that in order to believe me and know that it was you, Mary, the true mother of God, who was sending me, and ordering him to lodge you in a temple in such a deserted site, he would ask you for some signal, token, or sign to certify your will and convince him about my desire. I in full confidence left it to him to choose the sign he

---

[2]Ibid., p. 82.
[3]Ibid., pp. 83–84.

wanted . . . He left it to my care. With this I come to give you the reply; you should decide what you wish in this matter. It is up to you to give the sign, and up to me to carry it in your service."

With a friendly visage and grateful, endearing expressions, the most pure Queen of heaven, Mary, answered him, "Son Juan, tomorrow you are to see me, and I will give you such a sufficient sign that you will redeem your promise; they will receive you with applause and dismiss you with admiration. And note that such care, fatigue, and travel will not be lost sight of in relation to your advantage, nor forgotten in my gratitude. I will await you here; don't forget me."

(The bishop's spies)[1]

Juan left for his settlement without knowing or having noticed the concern that had arisen in the most illustrious lord don Juan de Zumárraga over such messages, the trustworthiness of the messenger, and the confidence with which he promised the signs he asked, for which reason he sent some servants from his house to follow Juan to the site he had designated and watch and spy on the person with whom he talked and conversed so that the experience of many eyes would be the guarantee of one tongue. With all care and caution they followed the way, always keeping our Juan in sight, and reached the bridge of Guadalupe, over its river, already close to the mountain. There before they realized it he disappeared from view and they lost sight of him, and although they tried to find him in that whole district, getting reports from various people, none helped, with which they returned, not only vexed, but enemies of Juan, discrediting him with the bishop and chilling his will, telling him what had happened, judging what the Indian asked to be deceit, fiction, or dream, proposing severe reprimands if perhaps he should come again and persist with his message.

(Fourth apparition)[2]

The following day, on which Juan was to return to carry the signs, went by, and he could not do so, because when he reached his settlement he found an uncle of his sick, and he busied himself in finding someone to give him medicines, which were of no use, because the sickness was aggravated and declared to be plague, among Indians with their native constitution an acute, contagious, and mortal disease. The second day after having been with the Virgin, he left his settlement very early in the morning to go to Santiago Tlatelolco to call a friar to administer the sacraments to the sick man. When he arrived in view of the site of the mountain of Guadalupe, although his

---

[1]IVM, p. 85.
[2]Ibid., pp. 86–89

usual way had always been along the slope looking west, he turned toward the one looking east, hoping to hasten his trip, because it was a matter that demanded quickness, and not to be delayed talking with the Virgin Mary; he thought that with that detour he could hide himself from her eyes, from the eyes of the most holy Mary, which see everywhere. Descending from the mountain where she was awaiting him, she came to meet him on his way.

Juan, whether saddened, shamed, or fearful, greeted her on his knees, bidding her good day. Returning his greeting, the compassionate Mother lovingly listened to his excuse, which was all the above; he also revealed his heart, telling her that he always intended to return the next day to obey her, be in her company, and serve her. The Virgin Mary, satisfied of the simple truth of the report, mercifully restored him to her favor, asking why he should be apprehensive of danger, fear diseases, or be afflicted by travails when he had her as his mother to see to his health and defense, with which he needed nothing else; that he should be relieved of all care, that he should not be held back by the sickness of his uncle, who was not in danger of death. She assured him that from that moment he was entirely sound, which was true, as was later established when they compared the times.

Juan Diego, consoled, pleased, and satisfied, put himself in her hands to send him wherever she thought best. Well may one praise the faith of this so recent Christian, since when the Virgin Mary said that his uncle was healthy, he did not doubt it, nor reply, and we know that once Christ celebrated the faith of one who trusted prudently in a similar situation.

It was now necessary, and the occasion obligatory, for the most holy Virgin Mary to fulfill Juan's promise and her word, providing sufficient signs for him to take to the most illustrious prince don Juan de Zumárraga. Juan, desirous of serving his mistress, the charitable Virgin, asked for and requested the sign that he was to take. Without any delay the Virgin Mary, pointing to the hill or mountain where she had called him and first imparted these matters to him, told him, "Climb this mountain to the same place where you saw me, spoke with me, and understood me, and from there cut, pick, and keep all the roses and flowers that you should discover and find; bring them back down to me."

Without replying that the time was December, in the frozen winter that destroys plants, without arguing that the mountain is by nature all flinty rocks and broken crags, without alleging his experience that in the times he had gone up at her call he had seen no roses or flowers, Juan with all haste and confidence ascended and climbed to the designated spot, where immediately there presented themselves to his eyes various flowers, put forth by miracle, born by prodigy, opened up by wonder, the roses inviting with their beauty, the white lilies bearing milk, the carnations blood, the violets zeal, the jasmines amber, the rosemaries hope, the other lilies love, and the brooms captivity, in anxious rivalry seeming to talk to his hands not only so that he would pick them, but take them first, through hidden impulses divining the glory for which they were being cut.

He picked them all, and collecting that spring of heaven, treasuring that garden of paradise in his rough, poor, humble cloak, clean indeed in its natural color, turning the two lower corners or ends up toward his chest and with his two hands and arms tying them up with the very knot hanging from his neck (that being the common style and costume of the Indians), he came down from the sacred mountain into the presence of the Virgin Mary, before whose eyes and into whose custody he put the roses and flowers picked by her command. The most holy Mother, taking them in her hands so that for a second time they should be miraculously reborn, regain fragrance, enliven in scent, and be freshly bedewed, returned and delivered them to him, telling him that those roses and flowers were the sign that he was to carry to the bishop, to whom on her behalf he should say that through them he should recognize the will of her who was making the request and the fidelity of him who was carrying them; he should report how she had commanded him to go up on that mountain to pick the flowers, and all the circumstances that he had observed, so that they all would oblige the prelate to carry out the construction of the temple that she was requesting.

Juan took his leave, and ever more enthusiastic, sure, and confidant, he went on his way to Mexico City, to the palace of his most illustrious lordship, always carrying the cloak with all care and veneration without daring to show it, or through neglect to drop it. Thus he arrived.

(Appearance of the image)[1]

With the flowers Juan entered the palace of the most illustrious lord don Juan de Zumárraga. He encountered his majordomo and some servants, whom he implored to advise the prelate that he wished to see him. No one took the effort to do so, whether it was early, or whether they already knew him, and without doubt they were all the more annoyed with his importunate petitioning because of the report of their companions who had spied on him. He waited a long time, and seeing his patient waiting, and that he gave indications of carrying something covered up and gathered in the cloak, they came over in curiosity to look into it, showing interest in what it could be. Since resistance was useless, Juan, fearing perhaps that they could upbraid him with words or mistreat him with deeds, could not deny them a look at

---

[1]IVM, pp. 91–93.

the roses. They were not without astonishment when they saw them, because the time of year alone demanded that much, and considering how fresh, colorful, and beautiful they were. Greedily each one of them tried to take one of the flowers, and having persisted three times, they could not; it appeared to them that they were painted, engraved, or woven on the snowy cloak. At that, if not the desire to get rid of our Juan, the astonishing novelty of what they had seen made them hasten to advise their master that that Indian who had come other times had come to see him, and they reported what they had experienced with some roses that he had claimed to be bringing to him, which they understood to be only apparent, sculptured or designed on the material of the cloak, which is the cape of the Indian nation.

The lord bishop, whose concern about such a punctual messenger had already been aroused by the singularity of what he requested, and had been heightened by what his people had then reported to him, ordered that they should summon him in all haste. He came into his presence with the humility customary for such a wish and in consideration of such supreme dignity. Having reviewed for him all that had happened in his comings, returns, and messages, he calmly, devoutly, and cautiously said to him, "Lord and father, consequent on your commands to me, in accordance with what you asked me, and in compliance with what you entrusted to me, I told my lady, Mary mother of God, that you were requesting from her a sign so that you would believe me and you would serve her by building her a house and temple where she is asking you for it, and that I had promised to bring it, since you had left it up to my will. Very lovingly she received your message, and accepted your agreement, arrangement, and bargain, for which reason having been ordered to return to her house and presence, I asked her for the promised sign. Without difficulty she offered it to me in these roses that I bring you, which she delivered to me by her own hand and put in this cloak, having instructed me and sent me to climb the mountain to the same place where she had always awaited me, been in my presence, and imparted these matters to me. [She told me] to pick with my own hand these roses, as I did, without being detained by the obvious experience I had, that that hill never produces flowers, but thistles, thorns, spines, or wild mesquite. When I reached the top, all was solved and turned to the opposite in my hands, for from a barren mountain it was transformed into a garden with a variety of flowers. She told me that I should offer them to you in her name—and so I do—and that in them you would have sufficient signs of her continued desires and my repeated truths.

He exposed the white cloak to offer the present of heaven to the fortunate bishop. The latter, anxious to receive it, saw in that cloak a holy forest, a miraculous spring, an abbreviated garden of roses, white lilies, carnations, other lilies, broom, jasmines, and violets, which on all falling from the cloak left painted on it the Virgin Mary mother of God in the holy image that today is preserved, kept, and venerated in her sanctuary of Guadalupe of Mexico City.

When the image was exposed, all knelt, remaining astonished in ecstasy, bewildered in astonishment, exalted in bewilderment, made tender in exaltation, rapt in tenderness, in contemplative raptures, in sweet contemplations, in happy sweetness, in mute happiness ...

The exemplary bishop wanted to be the obedient disciple of Saint Paul and grateful to Mary, because rising in all reverence, respect, and devotion, he untied the cloak from the shoulders of Juan, and taking possession of the holy image as the richest vestment of his pontifical robes, he took it to his retreat and oratory, adorning it as a lady of such grandeur required. . . . He directed that the following day Juan Diego should return to the site of Guadalupe to point out there the place where the Virgin Mary asked for her ermita. All obeyed, and went happily on their way ...

(Juan Bernardino)[1]

The diligent explorers returned pleased with their experiences, not only of the site, but of the circumstances of the event. They reported to their most illustrious prince that they had reached the place which Juan pointed out to them, and there carried out Christian observances ... They all went with Juan Diego to his settlement and house; there he had left dangerously ill his uncle, whom they found in perfect health. The two relatives rejoiced and compared notes on the blessed events. The uncle, called Juan Bernardino, confessed his gratitude, and said that the Virgin Mary mother of God had miraculously given him the health he enjoyed and received from her hand, mercifully attending him at his pillow at the same time that his nephew Juan Diego had gone out to call a friar and administrator of the sacraments. He noted that the most holy Lady had commanded him that when he should see the bishop he should report to him all that he had seen and experienced in the miracle of his health, and ask him in her name to give her the title of the Virgin Mary of Guadalupe [as embodied] in the image she offered him. For entire credibility he gave, aside from the health he evinced, exact, living, true details about the holy image, her painting. They left it for the report that the venerable Juan Bernardino was to give to his most illustrious lordship, for they brought him too into his presence. In God's love and with pastoral benevolence, for several days he lodged in his palace the two

---

[1]IVM, pp. 98–99.

Indians, unique benefactors of this New World, since they were possessors of the relic that we enjoy in our holy image.

(Display of the image)[2]

With the circumstances, the concerns and desires of the most illustrious bishop increased, and he decided, so that with all speed an ermita could be provisionally built, and the faithful would be encouraged to pay the cost with their donations, not precluding Christian generosity in the future, he should put the miraculous image before the public, as he did, removing it from his oratory in the palace, sure that he could firmly anticipate the payment, reward, and glory for having lodged it for that time in his house . . .

The holy image was placed in the cathedral; it became known in the city, and everyone was moved to the point of desiring a public view of such a new miracle, and devotion sent them all hastening in Christian crowds . . .

(Description of the image)[3]

The canvas and cloak on which, out of flowers, this holy image appeared painted is of a textile native to this country, for it alone enjoys the material of which it is made. It is a plant called maguey, so useful, beneficial, rare, and unique, that it seems that in it God condensed the whole world for the comfort of man, conceding him everything necessary for human life; there has been no lack of those interested enough to occupy themselves in writing about, recounting, and adducing all its properties. This plant is treated by the native Indians in order to be capable of being woven, the textiles turning out more or less fine according to the treatment, perhaps acquiring the appearance of coarse cotton, another type of textile also of this land. The proper name of this cloak in their language is *ayatl*, which the Indians wear, although experience teaches that it is the dress of the poor Indians, as has always been observed. The cloak is composed of two sections sewn together with cotton thread. I have noticed, observing with full attention and from very close, that when the seam and union of the two sections meets the face of the image, it turns left, leaving that space free and whole as far as the top. The entire extent of the cloak is today over two *varas* in length and more than one in width.

The image of the Virgin from the bottom of her foot to the place where her hair—which is very dark and parted in the middle—arises, is six palms and a span in stature. Her face is full and demure. Her eyebrows are very thin, her color light brunette, her attitude humble and loving. Her hands are joined, raised, and placed against the breast; this action begins at the waist,

---

[2]Ibid., pp. 99–100.
[3]Ibid., pp. 104–6.

in which she has a purple belt, which emerges and falls underneath her hands into the two ends of the knot it is tied with. She shows only the tip of her right foot, with a gray shoe.

Her robe is full length, in the light parts a very light pink, and in the dark parts a very dense carmine, embroidered with fine work of flowers closely spaced, and among them some jasmines; all this is golden and stands out on the red. As a clasp at her neck she has a golden oval, and within it a black circle, in the middle of which is seen a cross. The sleeves of the robe are round and loose, revealing as a lining a kind of grayish edging. She also shows a white interior robe, [with small bits of lacework], following her arms as far as the wrist, where her hands began, [where they are revealed].

Her veil is of a sky blue color, which begins covering her head without hiding her face, and unfolding as far as her feet; it is folded in some places, being much doubled and gathered between her arms. It is all outlined with gold, with a rather wide ribbon that serves as hem or border. Stars are scattered on it, not only on the head and upper part, but in the rest that she reveals. A royal crown sits on the veil, with points or merlons of gold on blue. At her feet is a half moon, whose half circle shows the points upward, and whose middle receives the body of the image. The whole image is as if in a niche or tabernacle, in the midst of a sun which forms rays, the distant ones yellow, the closer ones orange, as if clearest beams made of thinnest gold arose from the back of the image, some of them, which are wavy, larger than the others. All together they are a hundred in number, and of these, twelve surround her head and face, always flying upward, with the division so that fifty fall on each side of the image. The remainder of the canvas and cloak, in height as well as width, is painted as though in rather light colored clouds.

This whole painting is raised over an angel serving as the foundation for such a divine edifice. The angel is seen from the waist up, and the rest is hidden among the clouds as far as the lowest end of the cloak. He is of a polished beauty; he has a red robe with a golden button that closes it. His wings are of various colors, stretched and spread out, as are the angel's arms. With his right hand he is catching and collecting the end of the veil, which falls down over the body of the moon; this small bit shows three stars, which are included in the number given above. With his left hand he is touching and holding the end of the robe, which falls loose to there. The action that the angel displays is so anxious, lively, and pleased, that he appears to be saying that he carries that most holy image with all veneration and care.

(Reference to Remedios)[1]

You [the Virgin Mary] came to conquer this land, accompanying its valiant conquerors with your holy image of Los Remedios, which this city and kingdom worship on the mountain where today it has its ermita, and where after the conquest it was hidden and isolated for many years until you saw fit to reveal it to another humble Indian, who was the custodian of such a relic for many years.

(Removal of the image to the chapel)[2]

The most illustrious and reverend lord don Juan de Zumárraga, the moment he knew that the ermita was finished, discussed taking the holy image of Mary there. He consulted with the two cabildos; he arranged a general procession, assigning for it the second day of Christmas, Tuesday two weeks after the revelation of the image. . . . On this day the consecrated prince don Juan inaugurated, dedicated, and blessed the ermita and celebrated pontifical mass.

(Details on Juan Diego)[3]

The fortunate Juan Diego asked the prelate for permission to come from his settlement and live at the ermita, serving its patron. Permission was kindly given him, and he was careful to take the appropriate action. . . .

The happy end of our Indian Juan Diego: He served in this ermita with loving punctuality; he proceeded with exemplary customs; he lived with singular virtue; he died leaving glorious expectations of his salvation, based in a Christian fashion in the mercy and favors of Mary. He died after sixteen years of service . . .

Juan Diego left as heirs of all his property, symbolized by the cloak, the children of this land, its citizens and residents, who as in a perpetual entail attain through divine means the benefits and intercession of Mary by her miraculous image. But by my understanding, the particular intention of this sovereign lady was that she felt this cloak to be an efficacious instrument for those of his nation, the Indians, whom she wished to move, catch the fancy of, instruct, and favor in the faith of her son Christ.

(The spring)[4]

At the foot of the mountain, in the part looking east, where the highway is level, there is an admirable well, the main one for the place. It was here that the Virgin Mary came to meet Juan Diego, when he was trying to take

---

[1] IVM, p. 131.
[2] Ibid., pp. 158–59.
[3] Ibid., pp. 159, 164, 165.
[4] Ibid., p. 166.

a detour, and gave him the roses for her image. . . . It is naturally pro-
digious. Its waters are rather thick, pallid, and disturbed; they spring out
with such great violence that they rise almost a third [of a vara] from the
earth, forming a frizzled, full, spongy plume, which appears, from the noise
and projection of the waters, from their force, impetus, and abundance, that
it will soon flood that meadow, but all this movement resolves itself, and
this gushing torrent and noisy splashing reduces itself, to a thread of water
so thin and slender that it is hardly perceived as it slips away. Its waters
always stay undiminished, and its movements never change, for it is never
exhausted, nor diverted by the various exhalations of the earth, or the cracks
that open with the summer heat. Its waters are known through public
experience of cures, attributed to miracle, to be medicinal for various diseases.

(First miracle)[1]

For most holy Mary was reserved the excellence that she is always ef-
fecting virtuous and compassionate deeds, mercies, prodigies, marvels, and
miracles, as she has shown in this place and ermita, where God placed her
from the very day she took possession, for that day, which the Indians had
celebrated greatly, it happened that among the entertainments in the fashion
of their nation they formed and divided into two squadrons or troops of
Chichimecs, for so they call the Indians who practice the bow and arrow.
Unintentionally an arrow was let loose, and it pierced the neck of an Indian,
felling him with a mortal wound. Seeing the unfortunate event, with great
cries they carried him off and hurled him down dead in the presence of the
Virgin and her holy image in the inaugurated ermita, asking her for relief.
He easily received it, for when they removed the arrow, he came to, alive,
without harm or wound. Only the signs of where the arrow had penetrated
remained as witnesses of the miracle, which caused astonishment, rejoicing,
and devotion among the Indians. Without doubt the Virgin Mary through
her image wanted in this way to begin to gain the hearts of those recently
converted to the faith of her sacred son Jesus Christ.

(Second miracle)[2]

In the year of 1544 a strong *cocoliztli* and contagious plague flamed up
among the Indians, whose vehemence in a few days killed over twelve
thousand people in the settlements surrounding Mexico City. The friars of
Saint Francis with merciful concern arranged a devout procession of Indian
boys and girls, six or seven years old, and with them walked from the mon-

---

[1]IVM, p. 170.
[2]Ibid., p. 171.

astery of Santiago Tlatelolco to the ermita of our Lady of Guadalupe, where they made a devotional visit, supplication, and petition for relief in such an urgent public need. The following day the favor and intercession of most holy Mary, and the effect of the visit to her image, began to be felt, for it having been the common thing to bury a hundred dead bodies every day, from that day it was reduced to one or two, and in a brief time that fatal contagion of such an intense plague was entirely remedied. It was a very public miracle, engendering in all the Indians loving devotion to the miraculous image of Guadalupe.

(Third miracle)[3]

In the beginnings of the conversion of this New World, our Lady the Virgin Mary took special pains to lavish favors on the Indians, to gain their enthusiasm, instruct them, and attract them to the Catholic faith and to the shelter of her intercession, for we see that she delivered and revealed the two miraculous images which today we enjoy within view of Mexico City to two Indians, this one in the sanctuary of Guadalupe, and the other in that of Los Remedios. The image of Los Remedios appeared to an Indian named don Juan, who found it on the mountain where it has its ermita today. He removed it from the maguey where it was and took it home with him, and he had it there for many years, until for certain reasons it was moved to a small church at the foot of the mountain, in sight of the house of this Indian. He, after the passage of some time, fell gravely ill, without hope of life. On this occasion he asked his people to bring him to the ermita of our Lady of Guadalupe, at more than two leagues' distance from the other one. They charitably bore him in a litter and placed him in the presence of the Virgin, where she received him, smiling at him and speaking lovingly to him, and granting him the health he asked. She commanded him to return to his home, climb the mountain where he had found her, and in the same spot build her a humble ermita (for until then she had none), giving him complete instructions. He regained his health entirely, giving thanks to the Virgin in her miraculous image, and obeyed the command, so much to the pleasure of the Virgin, that the moment the ermita was finished, the most holy image of Los Remedios by itself climbed up to the altar where it is today. I refer to her history, which so reports it.

(Fourth miracle)[4]

A gentlemen named don Antonio de Carvajal set out from Mexico City for the settlement of Tulancingo accompanied by a youth who was his rela-

---

[3]Ibid., p. 172.
[4]Ibid., pp. 174–75.

tive. On the way the latter's horse bolted and went wild, carrying him a distance of half a league at full speed through ravines and stony places in a fit without his being able to halt. His companions ran in pursuit, presuming that of necessity he was not only dead but torn to bits by the impetus of such an unbridled beast. They found him hurled to the ground, one foot hanging from a stirrup, with the horse quiet, calm, and meek, bent down and its forelegs somewhat twisted. Amazed to see him alive and unhurt, they asked him about the wonder.

He replied that when they departed from Mexico City they had entered the holy ermita of our Lady of Guadalupe, which is on the way. They had prayed in the presence of the most holy image of Mary, and along the rest of the way they had brought to memory the miracles she had worked with those devoted to her, and chatted and conversed about the miraculous nature of that image. The talk and conversation was left strongly impressed on his soul, for which reason, when he found himself in that obvious danger and hopeless peril, in the most heartfelt way, with exclamations of his soul he had invoked the Virgin Mary of Guadalupe, remembering what he had heard. His emotion and invocation took effect so promptly that he saw the most holy Virgin come as she is painted in her image of Guadalupe and stop the horse by the reins, the beast obeying her with such reverence that the position in which they found him was kneeling and wanting to kiss the earth in the presence of the powerful Virgin, who saved him and freed him from a difficulty so without solution, except by her hand.

(Fifth miracle)[1]

A man was kneeling before the main altar of the holy ermita, praying to the image of the Virgin of Guadalupe, when the rope of a large and very heavy lamp, one of those hanging in front of her, tore and broke. It fell on the head of the devotee who was there, and although the blow according to the weight and the height was enough to take his life or give him a dangerous wound, it not only did not hurt him in any way, but the lamp in falling was not dented, nor did the glass break, nor did the oil spill, nor did the light go out, which caused great amazement in all those present, seeing so many miracles in one.

(Sixth miracle)[2]

Licentiate Juan Vásquez de Acuña, who was vicar of this holy ermita for many years, went up to the main altar to say mass on an occasion when all the lights in the church and its lamps had gone out, because that spot is so

---

[1]IVM, p. 175.
[2]Ibid., pp. 176–77.

battered by winds. The assistant went out to light a candle, and while awaiting it the priest saw that two shining rays of the sun in whose midst the miraculous image of the Virgin is placed flew to the two candles that were placed there on the altar and miraculously lit them, in view of other people who were present. The assistant returned with light, and finding the candles already lit, before anyone told him he knew that light had come by a miracle.

(Seventh miracle)[3]

How then could I write the history of the general flood of Mexico City, suffered in the years that all know, and so similar to the first deluge? . . . It was Tuesday the 25th of September that the flood had its beginning and the waters began to enter the city. Through it, from her hermita of Guadalupe, came the Virgin in her miraculous image, accompanying an afflicted and tormented crowd led by the most illustrious lord don Francisco Manso y Zúñiga, archbishop of Mexico, who arranged it. She was lodged that night in the palace of this prince, perhaps so she could see the house and place where she was reborn among the flowers and appeared painted in that cloak of hers, challenging her to take pity on her city and homeland. In the morning she was moved to the main altar of the cathedral, where she stayed the whole time of the flood, allowing the human diligence of those who were trying to remedy it to do everything that could possibly be done and going beyond that to try the impossible, until it reached the point of fainting, surrendering, and giving up, resolved to live perpetually in the midst of waters with canoes going back and forth, an attitude that in a short time would bring the city entirely to ruin. Then the defense and intercession of the Virgin was recognized, for bit by bit the waters went down, leaving the city dry, something that neither the passage of the years nor the execution of the projects had been able to achieve. A public cry went up acclaiming the miracle of the holy image. . . .

The most illustrious lord don Francisco Manso y Zúñiga, seeing Mexico City dry, offered to God another sacrifice especially dedicated to the holy image, restoring it to its ermita with all solemnity, ornament, and ingenuity. Sunday the 14th of May of 1634 he brought her out in procession from the cathedral, going along the street called the street of the clock as far as the church of St. Catherine the Martyr, where she was lodged the rest of the day. The following morning he continued, leaving and placing her in her sanctuary.

---

[3]Ibid., pp. 177–79.

Abbreviations[1]

AC   *Arte de la lengua mexicana*, by Horacio Carochi.

ANS   *The Art of Nahuatl Speech: The Bancroft Dialogues*, ed. and tr. by Frances Karttunen and James Lockhart.

DK   *An Analytical Dictionary of Nahuatl*, by Frances Karttunen.

DS   *Dictionnaire de la langue nahuatl*, by Remi Siméon.

HT   The *Huei tlamahuiçoltica*, by Luis Laso de la Vega, ed. by Feliciano Velázquez.

IVM   *Imagen de la virgen Maria, . . .* , by Miguel Sánchez, ed. by Lauro López Beltrán.

VM   *Vocabulario de la lengua castellana y mexicana y mexicana y castellana*, by fray Alonso de Molina.

---

[1]For details of the titles see the Bibliography.

Bibliography

Andrews, J. Richard. "Directionals in Classical Nahuatl." *Texas Linguistic Forum 18* (1981): 1–16.

Bautista, fray Juan. *Libro de los huehuehtlahtolli: Testimonios de la antigua palabra*. Facsimile of the work of 1600, with an introductory study by Miguel León-Portilla and a translation by Librado Silva Galeana. México: Comisión Nacional Conmemorativa del V Centenario del Encuentro de Dos Mundos, 1988.

Beristáin de Sousa, José Mariano. *Biblioteca hispanoamericana septentrional*. 5 vols. México: Ediciones Fuente Cultural, 1883.

Bierhorst, John, ed. and trans. *Cantares Mexicanos: Songs of the Aztecs*. Stanford: Stanford University Press, 1985.

Botturini Benaduci, Lorenzo. *Idea de una nueva historia general de la America Septentrional fundada sobre material copioso de figuras, symbolos, caractères, y geroglificos, cantares, y manuscritos de autores indios ultimamente descubiertos*. Madrid: Imprenta de Juan de Zunniga, 1746.

Brewer, Forrest, and Jean G. Brewer. *Vocabulario mexicano de Tetelcingo, Morelos*. 2d ed. México: Instituto Lingüístico de Verano, 1971.

Burkhart, Louise M. *The Slippery Earth: Nahua-Christian Moral Dialogue in Sixteenth-Century Mexico*. Tucson: University of Arizona Press, 1989.

_____. "The Cult of the Virgin of Guadalupe in Mexico." In *World Spirituality: An Encyclopedia History of the Religious Quest*. Ed. by Ewert Cousins. Vol. 4: *South and Meso-American Native Spirituality*. Ed. by Garry Gossen and Miguel León-Portilla. New York: The Crossroad Publishing Company, 1993.

Burrus, Ernest, S. J. *The Oldest Copy of the Nican Mopohua*. CARA Studies on Popular Devotion, 4. Guadalupan Studies, 4. Washington, D.C.: 1981.

_____. La copia más antigua del Nican Mopohua. *Histórica: Organo del Centro de Estudios Guadalupanos* (1986): 5–27.

Carochi, Horacio. *Arte de la lengua mexicana con la declaración de los adverbios della*. Facsimile of 1645 edition, with introduction by Miguel León-Portilla. México: Instituto de Investigaciones Filológicas, Instituto de Investigaciones Históricas, Universidad Nacional Autónoma de México.

Cawley, Martinus, O. C. S. O., *Guadalupe: From the Aztec Language*. Washington, D.C.: Center for Applied Research in the Apostolate.

CARA Studies on Popular Devotion, vol. 2: Guadalupan Studies, No. 7, December 1983.

Christian, William. *Apparitions in Late Medieval and Renaissance Spain.* Princeton, N.J.: Princeton University Press, 1981.

Conde, José Ignacio, and María Teresa Cervantes de Conde, "Nuestra Señora de Guadalupe en el arte," in *Album conmemorativo del 450 aniversario de las apariciones de Nuestra Señora de Guadalupe.*, pp. 124–26. México: Ediciones Buena Nueva, 1981.

Cuevas, Mariano, S. J. *Historia de la Iglesia en México.* 4 vols. Tlalpam, D. F.: Impr. del Asilo Patricio Sanz, 1921–1924.

De la Maza, Francisco. *El guadalupanismo mexicano.* México: Fondo de Cultura Económica, 1981.

De la Torre Villar, Ernesto, and Ramiro Navarro de Anda, eds. *Testimonios históricos guadalupanos.* México: Fondo de Cultura Económica, 1982.

Demarest, Donald, and Coley Taylor, eds. *The Dark Virgin, the Book of Our Lady of Guadalupe: A Documentary Anthology.* New York: Academy Guild Press, 1956 (reprinted 1959).

Fernández de Uribe, José Patricio. *Disertacion Historico-critica en que el autor del sermon que precede sostiene la celestial imagen de Maria Santísima de Guadalupe de México, . . . escribiase por el año de 1778.* México: Oficina de D. Mariano de Zúñiga y Ontiveros, 1801.

Florencia, Francisco de, S. J. *La estrella del norte del norte de Mexico . . .* Madrid: Imprenta de Lorenzo de San Martín, Impresor de la Secretaría de Estado y del Despacho Universal de Indias y de otras varias Oficinas de S. M., 1785.

García Icazbalceta, Joaquín. *Bibliografía mexicana del siglo XVI.* New edition by Agustín Millares Carlo. México: Fondo de Cultura Económica, 1954.

_____. "Carta al Ilmo. Sr. Arzobispo de México D. Pelagio Antonio de Labastida y Dávalos." In *Investigación histórica y documental sobre la aparición de la Virgen de Guadalupe de México*, pp. 21–70. México: Ediciones Fuente Cultural, n.d.

Garibay K., Angel María. *Historia de la literatura náhuatl.* 2 vols. México: Editorial Porrúa S. A., 1961.

Gibson, Charles. *The Aztecs Under Spanish Rule: A History of the Indians of the Valley of Mexico, 1519–1810.* Stanford: Stanford University Press, 1964.

Horcasitas, Fernando. *El teatro náhuatl.* México: Universidad Nacional Autónoma de México, 1974.

Karttunen, Frances. *An Analytical Dictionary of Nahuatl* (DK). Austin:

University of Texas Press, 1983.

Karttunen, Frances, and James Lockhart, eds. and trans. *The Art of Nahuatl Speech: The Bancroft Dialogues* (ANS). UCLA Latin American Studies, 65. Los Angeles: UCLA Latin American Center Publications, 1987.

Key, Harold, and Mary Ritchie de Key. *Vocabulario mejicano de la Sierra de Zacapoaxtla, Puebla*. México: Instituto Lingüistico de Verano, 1953.

Lamadrid, Jesús Galera. *Nican mopohua: Breve análisis literario e histórico*. México: Editorial Jus, 1991.

Lasso (Laso) de la Vega, Luis. *HVEI TLAMAHVIÇOLTICA* . . . México: Imprenta de Juan Ruiz, 1649.

_____. *HVEI TLAMAHVICOLTICA* . . . [*sic*] (HT) Ed. and trans. by Primo Feliciano Velázquez. Academica Mexicana de Santa María. México: Carreño e hijos, editores, 1926.

_____. *Nican mopohua*. Ed. and trans. by Mario Rojas Sánchez. México: Imprenta Ideal, 1978.

_____. *La aparición de Santa María de Guadalupe*. Facsimile of the earlier Velázquez edition of *HVEI TLAMAHVIÇOLTICA* . . . México: Editorial Jus, 1981.

León-Portilla, Ascensión H. de. *Tepuztlahcuilolli: Impresos en náhuatl, historia y bibliografía*. Vol. 1. México: Universidad Nacional Autónoma de México, 1988.

Lockhart, James. *Nahuas and Spaniards: Postconquest Central Mexican History and Philology*. Stanford, Calif., and Los Angeles: Stanford University Press and UCLA Latin American Center Publications, 1991.

_____. *The Nahuas After the Conquest: A Social and Cultural History of the Indians of Central Mexico, Sixteenth through Eighteenth Centuries*. Stanford: Stanford University Press, 1992.

_____. "A Double Tradition: Editing Book Twelve of the Florentine Codex." In *Critical Issues in Editing Exploration Texts*, ed. by Germaine Warkentin. Toronto: University of Toronto Press, 1995.

_____, ed. and tr. *We People Here: Nahuatl Accounts of the Conquest of Mexico*. Berkeley and Los Angeles: University of California Press, 1993.

Mendieta, fray Gerónimo de, O. F. M. *Historia eclesiástica indiana*. 3rd edition, in facsimile. México: Editorial Porrúa, S. A., 1971.

Molina, fray Alonso de, O. F. M. *Vocabulario de la lengua castellana y mexicana y mexicana y castellana* (VM). México: Editorial Porrúa, S. A., 1977.

Nebel, Richard. *Santa María Tonantzin Virgen de Guadalupe: Religiöse*

Kontinuität und Transformation in Mexiko. Immensee: Neue Zeitschrift für Missionswissenschaft, 1992.

———. *Santa María Tonantzin Virgen de Guadalupe: Continuidad y transformación religiosa en México* (translation of Nebel 1992). México: Fondo de Cultura Económica, 1995.

Noguez, Xavier. *Documentos guadalupanos: Un estudio sobre las fuentes de información tempranas en torno a las mariofanías en el Tepeyac*. México: Fondo de Cultura Económica, 1993.

Nueva colección de documentos para la historia de México. Cartas de religiosos de Nueva España, 1539–1594. Ed. by Joaquín García Icazbalceta. 3 vols. México: Editorial Chávez Hayhoe, 1941.

O'Gorman, Edmundo. *Destierro de sombras: luz en el origen y culto de Nuestra Señora de Guadalupe de Tepeyac*. México: Universidad Nacional Autónoma de México, 1986.

Ortiz de Montellano, Guillermo. *Nicān mopouha* [sic]. México: Universidad Iberoamericana, Departamento de Ciencias Religiosas, Departamento de Historia, 1990.

Peterson, Jeannette Favrot. "The Virgin of Guadalupe: Symbol of Conquest or Liberation?" *Art Journal* (Winter 1992): 39–47.

Poole, Stafford. *Our Lady of Guadalupe: The Origins and Sources of a Mexican National Symbol, 1531–1797*. Tucson: University of Arizona Press, 1995.

Rojas Sánchez, Mario, ed. *Nican mopohua. Dn. Antonio Valeriano, traducción del náhuatl al castellano por el presbítero Mario Rojas Sánchez*. México: Imprenta Ideal, 1978.

Ruiz de Alarcón, Hernando. *Treatise on the Heathen Superstitions that Today Live Among the Indians Native to this New Spain*. Ed. and tr. by J. Richard Andrews and Ross Hassig. Norman: University of Oklahoma Press, 1984.

Sahagún, fray Bernardino de. *Florentine Codex: General History of the Things of New Spain*. Tr. by Arthur J. O. Anderson and Charles E. Dibble. 13 parts. Salt Lake City and Santa Fe, N.M.: University of Utah Press and School of American Research, Santa Fe, 1950–82.

———. *Historia general de las cosas de la Nueva España . . .* Ed. by Angel María Garibay K. México: Editorial Porrúa, 1981.

Sánchez, Miguel. *Imagen de la virgen Maria, Madre de Dios de Guadalupe. Milagrosamente aparecida en la ciudad de Mexico. Celebrada en su historia, con la profecia del capitulo doce del Apocalipsis*. México: Imprenta de la Viuda de Bernardo Calderón, 1648.

———. *Imagen de la virgen Maria, . . .* (IVM). In *La primera historia gua-*

dalupana impresa, ed. by Lauro López Beltrán. Obras guadalupanas de Lauro López Beltrán, 4. México: Editorial Tradición, 1981.

Sigüenza y Góngora, don Carlos de. *Piedad heroyca de don Fernando Cortes.* Ed. by Jaime Delgado. Colección Chimalistac de libros y documentos acerca de la Nueva España, 7. Madrid: José Porrúa Turanzas, Editor, 1960.

Siller A., Clodomiro I. *La evangelización guadalupana.* Cuadernos de Estudios Indígenas, 1. México: CENAMI, December, 1984.

Siméon, Remi. *Dictionnaire de la langue nahuatl.* Graz: Akademische Druck- u. Verlagsanstalt, 1963.

Torquemada, fray Juan de, O. F. M. *Monarquía indiana.* Facsimile. 3 vols. México: Editorial Porrua, S. A., 1969.